Studies in Economic Ethics and Philosophy

Studies in Economic Ethics and Philosophy

P. Koslowski (Ed.)
Ethics in Economics, Business, and Economic Policy
192 pages. 1992

P. Koslowski · Y. Shionoya (Eds.)
The Good and the Economical
Ethical Choices in Economics and Management
212 pages. 1993

Hans De Geer (Ed.)

Business Ethics in Progress?

With 8 Figures and 15 Tables

Springer-Verlag

Berlin Heidelberg New York
London Paris Tokyo
Hong Kong Barcelona
Budapest

Professor Dr. Hans De Geer
FA Institute for Research on Business & Work
P.O.Box 5042
S-10241 Stockholm, Sweden

ISBN-13:978-3-642-78865-9 e-ISBN-13:978-3-642-78863-5
DOI: 10.1007/978-3-642-78863-5

Softcover reprint of the hardcover 1st edition 1994

42/2202-543210 - Printed on acid - free paper

Preface

Business ethics is increasingly paid attention to in the public debate. The rapid changes in business conditions, due to changing institutions, changing markets and new means of communication in business, call for a renewal of the discussion of ethics and morality in business life. Among many other things, the questions of equality of race, religion and gender, of environmental conditions for sustainable industrial growth and the necessity to supply meaningful jobs for the young generation call for ethical consideration as an integrated part of the decision-making processes in business and society. The number of corporations and firms and of public bodies, that have written ethical codes and other instituted means of enhancing corporate ethics, is increasing. Business schools all around the world include business ethics in their curriculum.

In this development scholars from different academic fields have contributions to make. The interest in business ethics is not restricted to ethicists and economists. Also researchers from other areas, like sociology, history and theology, join in the efforts. As an academic discipline of its own, if it is to be regarded as such, business ethics is a remarkably creative arena for exchange of ideas from different corners of the learned world. It is now our task to develop this sometimes confusing blend into a useful resource for the further moralising debate.

The European Business Ethics Network (EBEN) has since 1989 assembled the European research institutes in the field for annual meetings. The papers and discussions from the 1991 meeting, which was hosted by the Research Institute for Philosophy at Hannover, Germany, were published by Springer-Verlag 1992 in the volume *Ethics, Economics, Business and Economic Policy*, edited by Professor Peter Koslowski.

In 1992 the "4th Annual EBEN Meeting of Business Ethics Research Centers in Europe" was arranged by the FA Institute, Stockholm. In this volume the papers presented at this meeting at Stockholm in May 1992 are published, demonstrating the wide range of current topics within business ethics research, from the theoretical arguments in papers like those of van Luijk and Petersen, over the descriptive and quantitative studies by Brytting and Bergkvist to the report by De Geer from a case of implementing an ethical code. At this meeting special attention was given to the situation in East Europe. Papers by Nemçova, Fekete and

Rokitiansky demonstrate in different ways the ethical dimensions in the ongoing discussions, in the actual reforms and in the obstacles for change of business life in the former communist countries.

I would like to thank EBEN and its president, Professor Henk van Luijk, for the opportunity to invite colleagues from all over Europe to the Stockholm meeting. I would also like to thank the participants in the vivid discussions – so vivid in fact that they could not easily be summarized here – and my co-workers at the FA Institute for their efforts in making the conference a success.

Stockholm, December 1993 Hans De Geer

Contents

CONTENTS

Part Two

Reports from the Field

CONTENTS

Part One

Towards an Understanding of Business Ethics

Chapter 1

Rights and Interests in a Participatory Market Society*

HENK VAN LUIJK

Introduction

In a recent article on cooperation Robyn Dawles and Richard Thaler present the following observation:

> In the rural areas around Ithaca it is common for farmers to put some fresh products on a table by the road. There is a cash box on

* I have presented earlier versions of (parts of) this paper at the 1er Symposium International Éthique, Économie et Entreprise, Paris 1989; at the Annual Meeting of the Society for Business Ethics, Washington D.C. 1989; at the Second Annual Conference of EBEN, the European Business Ethics Network, Barcelona 1989; at the Forschungsinstitut für Philosophie, Hannover 1991; at the Fourth Annual Conference of EBEN, London 1991, and at INSEAD, Fontainebleau 1992. I have written the penultimate version during a stay as Visiting Scholar at the Center for Business Ethics, Bentley College, Waltham MA and at the Fletcher School for Law and Diplomacy of Tufts University, Medford MA during the Fall semester of 1991, and presented it in a public lecture at Bentley College as well as at the Wharton School, University of Pennsylvania, Philadelphia PA. Discussions at all those occasions have helped me greatly in clarifying the argument. The penultimate version also has been thoroughly discussed with the participants in the Research Programma 'Emancipation and Rationality' at the University of Groningen and with the members of the EBEN Executive Committee, Brussels. All those people, as well as Tom Donaldson, Georgetown University, Washington D.C. deserve my sincere gratitude for their very valuable comments.

> the table, and customers are expected to put money in the box in return for the vegetables they take. The box has just a small slit, so money can only be put in, not taken out. Also, the box is attached to the table, so no one can (easily) make off with the money. We think that the farmers who use this system have just about the right model of human nature. They feel that enough people will volunteer to pay for the fresh corn to make it worthwhile to put it out there. The farmers also know that if it were easy enough to take the money, some would do so.[1]

The farmers of Ithaca introduce us into a domain, characterised by landmarks like 'money', 'self-interest', 'mixed motives' and 'reciprocal expectations', a domain that is worth entering and exploring. My argument, located within this domain, runs as follows: "The market, as the realm of money-bound for-profit transactions, constitutes a basic human institution that deserves thorough moral scrutiny. Today, however, the **ethics of the market place**, commonly called 'business ethics', is dangerously flawed by a systematic underestimation of mixed motives in general and of self-interest especially, and by neglecting moral opportunities found in the sphere of public/private initiatives. Therefore the agenda of present-day business ethics must be altered accordingly."

The argument is related to three ongoing discussions in social ethics: first, the discussion about motives people have when engaging in actions that obviously affect others as well, and about intentions as distinct from motives, second, the discussion about egoism and altruism as basic patterns of social action, and the question whether there is something in between that deserves moral attention, and third, the discussion about the difference between prudential and moral actions, between prudence and morality as basic categories in social ethics. The topics of the three discussions are not identical, but neither are they totally divergent. Probably this is one of the reasons why confusion in these realms is so persistent. In what follows I do not pretend to dissipate all ambiguities. But the sheer knowledge that fog is ahead is often sufficient to make us proceed carefully.

I develop my argument in three steps:

1. The rehabilitation of self-interest in modern culture
2. Action patterns, claims and interests: a typology
3. Ethics in a participatory market society.

---

1 Robyn M. Dawes and Richard H. Thaler: "Cooperation", *Journal of Economic Perspectives* (1988), 2, p. 195. Quoted in: Jane J. Mansbridge (Ed.): *Beyond Self-interest*, Chicago/London (The University of Chicago Press) 1990, p. xiii.

I. The Rehabilitation of Self-Interest in Modern Culture

1. A Short History of Self-Interest[2]

Christianity knew it, Immanuel Kant knew it, everybody seems to know it: avarice is sin, greed is one of the three basic human vices next to ambition and lust for domination, and money is the root of all evil. What everybody does not know is that, somewhere in the seventeenth and eighteenth century, a rehabilitation of self-interest came about, that has kept the concept, up to today, in a sort of balance between suspicion and permission.

To make self-interest less repugnant, one way is to compare it to something overtly more distasteful. That is exactly what Montesquieu did, the eighteenth century French philosopher and political theorist. Albert Hirschman has the story, in a brilliant essay entitled: *The Passions and the Interests. Political Arguments for Capitalism before Its Triumph*[3]. He sketches how, in the seventeenth and eighteenth century, interest was looked upon favorably, because it was considered to be "a relatively peaceful and harmless alternative to the violent passion for glory which had long inspired the military, aristocratic, and landed ruling classes of Europe, (...) [classes driven by] an ideal that often had bloody and destructive consequences, that had painful or even fatal externalities for the bystanders of glorious escapades"[4]. He refers to a key sentence of Montesquieu who says: "It is almost a general rule that wherever manners are gentle [moeurs douces] there is commerce; and wherever there is commerce, manners are gentle"[5]. And he comments: "There is here, then, the insistent thought that a society where the market assumes a central position for the satisfaction of human wants will not only produce considerable new wealth because of the division of labor and consequent technical progress, but generate as a by-product, or external economy, a more 'polished' human type – more honest, reliable, orderly, and disci-

2 See STEPHEN HOLMES: "The Secret History of Self-Interest", in: JANE MANSBRIDGE: *Beyond Self-Interest*, pp. 267–286.

3 ALBERT O. HIRSCHMAN: *The Passions and the Interests. Political Arguments for Capitalism before Its Triumph*, Princeton, New Jersey (Princeton University Press) 1977. See also A. O. HIRSCHMAN: *Rival Views of Market Society and Other Recent Essays*, New York (Viking) 1986.

4 STEPHEN HOLMES: "The Secret History of Self-Interest", pp. 275–276, commenting upon Hirschman's thesis.

5 HIRSCHMAN (1986), p. 107.

plined, as well as more friendly and helpful, ever ready to find solutions to conflicts and a middle ground for opposed opinions"[6].

Experts tell us that, today, manners among merchants of coffee and tea are strikingly more gentle than in the petro-chemical industry. However that may be, it seems safe to say that, ever since the times of Montesquieu, the idea of commerce and market transactions being compatible with common moral decency has been part of modern conscience. In a sense, the taming of the passions by balanced commercial interests implied the taming of self-interests as well.

Besides, the idea of self-interest has a basic democratic and egalitarian power. Not everybody is endowed with hereditary privileges, not every person can afford to have violent passions, but everyone has interests[7]. In that respect, at least, we are all equal. This, however, faces us now with the philosophical question: what exactly do we have, when we have interests?

II. Action Patterns, Claims and Interests: a Typology

1. Motive and Structure

In recent times, innumerable experiments have been set up in laboratories of psychology and organizational theory that test subjects with choices between self-rewarding behavior and the interests of others. It commonly appears that a solid 25 to 35% refuses to take self-interested action at the expense of the group. The motive for this behavior usually is worded as: 'Doing the right thing'. It also appears that the level of cooperative conduct can be raised up to 85% by allowing discussion and other procedures that increase feelings of group identity. The level of self-interested actions can be increased by raising the payoff, and by using students of economics[8].

What the experimenters want to investigate is the set-up of people's motives and incentives. Cynics don't need experiments to contend that

6 HIRSCHMAN (1986), p. 109.

7 STEPHEN HOLMES, *l. c.*, p. 283.

8 See JANE MANSBRIDGE: "The Rise and Fall of Self-Interest in the Explanation of Political Life", in: J. MANSBRIDGE: *Beyond Self-Interest*, pp. 3–22, esp. p. 17.

"basically, human behavior is motivated by self-interest". But this thesis is provably false, for every now and then people show clear examples of altruistic behavior, inside and outside laboratory situations. In those cases the defender will take refuge in the word 'basically': "On second inspection, you'll find that, subconsciously, all human behavior has self-interest as its decisive motive. Ultimately, the unselfish hero is brave and self-sacrifying because she **wants** to be so, because she gets some **reward** from being so". With the appeal to unconscious motives being kept open indefinitely, the thesis **never** can be proved to be incorrect. Refusing to accept whatever kind of facts as valid refutation, the theory is properly irrefutable. Popper has taught us that an irrefutable theory is extremely boring. So let us forget about the cynic, and concentrate on what really is at stake. What does it mean that people, although not always, have self-interested motives every once in a while?

It means that the structure of human action can be **self-directed** as well as **other-directed**. But clearly, this reply uses the philosopher's trick of answering the question by changing the subject. The question was about motives, the answer is about structures. Are there good reasons for this switch in attention?

There are indeed. For motives often are hard to untie, whereas structures can be reconstructed. Years ago, when I was a student, a professor of mine impressed me indelibly, by stating almost casually: "The real motive of our actions is always unconscious". I have carried this sentence with me ever since. At that time he didn't offer much of an explanation, but gradually I figured out what I now think he wanted us to understand. An action can have, and often has, several motives simultaneously, clear as well as confused ones, high-minded and trivial, overtly selfish next to unselfish, motives that change places during the course of the action, and that, at the same time, are irreducible to each other as well as to the **one** motive that, in an unreflected but powerful way, is always present underneath: to survive. The person who is capable of untying the Gordian knot of human motives, truly deserves, as the Oracle says, to be the King of Asia.

Not called to be a monarch, we nonetheless succeed in reconstructing, not the motives but the **basic structure** of our actions and those of others. Sure, it may be hard to reconstruct every single act. But often we are quite able to grasp the **pattern**, the **intentional structure** present in a sequence of actions and, retrospectively, in single actions within it. We then may discover that, with regard to their basic structure, human actions fall into one out of three possible categories. I call them: **self-directed**, **other-including** and **other-directed actions**[9].

At the background here is a distinction, subtle but real, between **motives** and **intentions**. Motives are all incentives and drives to action, of whatever nature, that incite someone to act in a certain way. Greed can be a motive, and lust for power, but so can honesty, compassion and a sense of duty. The same professor I quoted earlier defined a motive as 'an antecedent that is active by its meaning', the emphasis being on 'active', in the sense of a **causa efficiens**. Intentions, on the other hand, are of the nature of a **causa finalis**, the indirect incitement that goes with the setting of a goal and the subsequent identification with the goal set. Motives often are intertwined, and resistant to analysis, whereas intentions, by their partly reflective nature, lend themselves to be grasped and reconstructed, at least to a large extent, by the actor as well as by the impartial observer. It is not surprising that ethical analysis feels more at ease with intentions than with motives, the realm of intentions being more suited to moral judgements concerning liability and responsibility than the shimmering realm of motives. Now what is it that, from a moral perspective, **a taxonomy of the intentional structure of action patterns** can make us aware of? In order to answer that question we first have to ask what the typology of self-directed, other-including and other-directed actions stands for.

A **self-directed** action is an action that intends the actor and the recipient of the benefits of the action to coincide. The outcome of the action returns in total to the actor. The designing of a career path is a self-directed action, and so is an investment made at the stock market, or the decision to sue – or not to sue – your dentist.

An **other-including** action is an action in which the actor intends to share with others the position of being the recipient of the action's benefits. The action is designed so as to yield results for more than only the actor, whereby the amount and the quality of the results need not be the same for all recipients. The signing of a labor contract is an other-including action, for next to payment, security and job-satisfaction for the actor the action yields also labor force and loyalty to the benefit of the employer. So is the opening of a plant in a low-wages country, to the extent that the action intends to bring profit to the corporation and wages to the country, - low wages, maybe, but wages nonetheless.

9 For brevity's sake, I shall speak only of an 'action' in the singular, acknowledging that, to get hold of a single action, we frequently need the detour via the action *pattern* of which it is part.

An **other-directed** action, finally, is an action with which the actor intends results that exclusively benefit another or others than himself or herself. Non-reciprocated gift-giving is an other-directed action, or giving a failing employee a second last chance, and so is joining Amnesty International or Green Peace in their activities. Some religious, political or ideological groups are almost exclusively committed to other-directed actions. Now, as we saw, the cynic bluntly denies that such actions are at all possible, because he confuses the **basic direction** of an action and its **accompanying experiences**. The true part of his thesis is that, the more an action is real, the more we want it to be earmarked as ours, and the more we enjoy that, by doing what we do, we are able to be the person we want to be. This counts for other-directed actions as well as for self-directed and other-including ones. These accompanying feelings, however, do not change the basic direction of the action. Or, to put it negatively, in the long run it always **shows** whether people – or corporations – really intend their actions to be other-directed, or whether they let the accompanying feelings of self-affirmation take the lead, and, by doing so, in fact are cheating others and themselves[10].

What we have here is a modest model of the basic directions an actor can intend his actions to possess. The model may be descriptively satisfying. However, it is strikingly incomplete where it comes to a **moral evaluation** of human actions. For then **interests and claims** have to be taken into account as well. In a somewhat exaggerated form one might even say: ethics is about claims and interests as much as it is about intentions. By 'interest' I mean an advantage that someone is able to pursue or, once attained, wants to protect, and by 'claim' I mean a justifiable demand from somebody for something as due – ethicists may want to call it a 'right', but, for the time being, I prefer the broader concept of 'claim'.

Now what happens if we combine the model of the types of action with the basic moral concepts of claims and interests?

2. Claims and Interests

Nothing much happens with regard to **other-directed** actions. The description just gets somewhat more precise, as it becomes clear that,

10 The thesis that "in the long run it shows", negatively when the actor is simulating altruism, positively when he is not, is pivotal in ROBERT FRANK: *Passions Within Reason*, New York (W. W. Norton & Co.) 1988.

when talking about an other-directed action, we are talking about an actor – individual or group – that intends its action to be totally directed toward the fostering of the **interests** of others, without, however, these others being **entitled to demand that** the actor do so. The uses of the concepts of 'interests' and 'claims' shows that, morally speaking, other-directed actions stand for what commonly are called **altruistic** actions: highly respectable and applaudable from a moral point of view, but not to be considered a moral **duty**. Acts of love, signs of solidarity, precious contributions to the common good – call them whatever seems appropriate, but don't call them duties or obligations. The employer is not morally **obliged** to grant the failing employee a second last chance, but if he does he deserves moral appreciation, not only from the employee but also from the wider community[11].

Self-directed actions need more comment from a moral point of view. We described them as actions in which the outcome of the action is intended to return in total to the actor. This intention, however, does not exclude that others are **affected** by the action. They are not intentionally **included**, but they are touched nonetheless. Parents often strongly identify themselves with the career path of their children. In many Western countries, however, children are not morally obliged to model their career according to their parents' wishes. Parents ultimately cannot require their grown-up children to accomodate to their preferences. In this sense, the self-directed action of the child designing its career path is unchallenged by legitimate moral claims.

There are, in effect, **three moral possibilities** in the confrontation of self-directed actions and claims of others. A self-directed action can remain unchallenged by legitimate moral claims. In this case, the appropriate moral attitude of the actor can be conceived as part of an **ethics of self-development**, in accordance with the Aristotelian prescription: Be who you are. The basic ethical principle here is the **principle of fidelity to one's own capacities**: develop the talents nature and upbringing have endowed you with.

11 JANE MANSBRIDGE uses a wider definition: "By unselfish or altruistic behavior, I mean (...) behavior promoting another's welfare that is undertaken for a reason independent of its effects on one's own welfare. That reason can include both duty and love, both commitment to a moral principle regardless of its effects on the welfare of others, and moral or empathetic concern with the welfare of others", *Beyond Self-Interest*, p. 142. I can imagine *unselfish* behavior to be described so broadly. But I have difficulty in denoting behavior as *altruistic* in cases in which not the slightest mentioning seems to be made of others as recipients of the behavior.

In the case, however, where a corporation opens a plant in a low-wages country and intends, in a self-directed way, to keep the wages as low as possible, the workers legitimately may challenge this behavior by claiming that not only wages are paid, but **fair** wages. In these cases, the challenge implies that, from a moral point of view, the action cannot be defined as exclusively self-directed. Here two possibilities present themselves. The company either can reject the claim, legitimate as it may be. The ethical qualification for such a reaction is **egoism**, conceived as a pattern of exclusively self-directed actions, negating or explicitly rejecting whatever legitimate claim at stake. Or the company may recognize the well-foundedness of the claim and act accordingly, notwithstanding real costs involved. By so doing it enters the realm of what I will call in a moment a **recognitional ethics**.

It is the **class of other-including actions** that requires the most elaborate comment. Here several varieties of a combination of other-includingness, and interests and claims of included agents deserve moral attention.

a) Transactional Ethics

One important variety obtains in situations in which the parties, included in the action pattern, have **common interests** and roughly **equal claims**. The situation typically occurs in **market** transactions, but may equally occur in the courtroom or at the negotiation table.

Here, however, a conceptual clarification is due, the concept of 'common interests' being inadmissibly vague and fluid. I can think of three different situations in which individuals or groups are said to pursue common interests.

In the **first** situation people are found to have **simultaneous** interests. It is, in a way, the thinnest form of common interests. What agents have in common here is not a specific interest but the mere fact of being a pursuer of particular interests that happen to coincide in time. The environmental movement and the government want to reduce the CFC emission in order to prevent the greenhouse effect from spreading ever more, and the petrochemical industry wants to enter the market of unleaded petrol. A question of simple coincidence, one might say. The moral requirements that go with it are equally simple. Here agents only are morally required to adhere to the **principle of equality**, stating that every agent should permit every other to be active as well, allowing her the same amount of freedom of action he claims for himself, without feeling obliged, however, to foster the interests of the other. Entering the market of unleaded petrol doesn't imply the obligation to contribute to the raising of the environmental awareness of speeding drivers. In terms of game theory one might speak of a 'no sum game', because the effects of the different actions are not fit to be added, nor do they need to be. The equality at stake here is of a rather abstract nature: not equality of endowments, nor equality in power, but only equality in possessing the position of all being pursuers of interests.

In a **second** situation common interests are at stake in that the interests of the various agents are **connected** in such a way that the interest of the one cannot be realized without the interest of the other being satisfied as well, at least to a certain degree. Everybody in the situation has interests that can only be pursued effectively if everyone is prepared to engage in **cooperative arrangements** that yield a **social surplus**. By contributing to the cooperative venture, and accepting the restraints that go with it, all parties play a role in the production of mutual advantages. People recognize that more can be achieved than the sum of what each is able to acquire for herself on the basis of self-directed actions. This 'more', however, this social surplus, requires the commitment to a pursuit of the interests of the other as well as of one's own. It requires the simultaneous recognition of the other as equally entitled to claim that everybody in the cooperative arrangement can count upon the honesty and trustworthiness of the others and can legitimately presume that the others will refrain from free-riding. The farmers of Ithaca know what we are talking about.

People engage in a commercial transaction for the profit they expect from it. This profit cannot be made if there is not an equivalent profit to be gained by one or more cooperating others. To gain the cooperative surplus the parties involved are reciprocally indispensable, and are equally entitled to an appropriate share in the outcome of the arrangement to which each has voluntarily committed herself. Every normal market transaction can serve as an example of such a situation. I want to have my house painted, but I lack the expertise and the equipment to do it myself, for the house is high and it has some difficult corners. The painting firm I contact has both the equipment and the expertise, but needs my order to be able to use them and to make money out of them. Once we have found one another the painter better makes sure to apply the right quality of paint at all the places we agreed, for otherwise, once I discover his untrustworthiness, I never will call upon him anymore, and I may even be able to damage his reputation to quite some extent by spreading the information about his poor performance. And I, in turn, better make sure to pay the firm the sum I rightly owe them within the thirty days we agreed on, for otherwise I may run into quite some trouble and may in the future have some difficulties in finding somebody willing to paint my house or to repair my water supply. Collaborating as we agreed to do, however, we both contribute to the Gross National Product on the general level, and we generate mutual advantages at the personal level. In such a situation the moral bottom line is marked by some principles of a primarily **procedural** nature, indicating how the win-win game should be played. I mention the **principle of honesty**, implying that one should operate in good faith, fairly and equitably, not betraying the confidence received, and the **principle of reciprocity**, implying that one should avoid free-riding on somebody else's efforts – principles that, at least, help to avoid unnecessary transaction costs, and that, taken together, constitute the basics of **the morality of the marketplace**. Other-including actions based upon either simultaneous or connected interests and equal claims are acceptable from a moral point of view when people **agree to be moral** according to the principles of a market morality, the principles of equality, honesty and reciprocity. This is why the resulting type of morality sometimes is referred to as 'morals by agreement'[12].

We face here a very interesting class of actions, in which rational self-interest, respect for the claims and interests of others, exchange transactions, and a specific type of morality coincide. In its fully elaborated form this type of market morality leads to what I might call a **'transactional ethics'**, as a specific type of ethics, well-suited for relations in the market place. Right now we may notice that the rehabilitation of self-interest, inaugurated in the eighteenth century, apparently was the rehabilitation, not of self-directed actions, but of other-including actions based on common, that is simultaneous or connected, interests and equal claims. The rehabilitation of self-interest, from a moral point of view, is **the rehabilitation of market morality**.

---

12 In his book *Morals by Agreement,* Oxford (Clarendon Press) 1986, DAVID GAUTHIER has presented a first elaboration of the principles of a market morality and the conditions under which such a morality might arise.
Recently, NORMAN BOWIE has treated the concept of market morality in: "New Directions in Corporate Social Responsibility", *Business Horizons*, 34 (July–August 1991), 4, pp. 56–65.

b) Participatory Ethics

There is a **third** situation in which common interests are at stake, now understood as **shared interests**. Here individuals and groups, including governmental agencies, cooperate in order to produce a single much desired effect, without participants being morally **obliged** to contribute, and none of the parties being entitled to claim the efforts of the other. As long as corporations are not forced by law, they can decide for themselves whether they hire a substantial number of immigrant workers, set up special training programmes, and adapt production processes accordingly. By choosing to do so, they join with the **intentions** of governmental agencies and immigrant groups alike, namely the integration of immigrants in the national culture and society, although **motives** to take part in such a project may differ. The corporation may want to avoid becoming subject to legal prescriptions – the motive behind much self-regulation of corporations. It may need workers anyhow. It may, for humanitarian or community reasons, or just for the reason of decency, want to be part of the project. Often motives will prove to be mixed, and there is nothing morally wrong with that. The important thing is that various people and groups gather around a common, shared interest, that without their joined cooperation would not get off the ground. They are in no way forced to cooperate, they join voluntarily, **commiting themselves** to, what I might call, a **non-enforceable obligation**, on the basis of a kind of **reciprocal altruism**.

Let me give a more elaborated example. It is located in The Netherlands, a society I happen to be familiar with. But I am sure that similar experiences can be reported from other regions as well[13].

It is about a project called 'Coast Location Plan Southern Holland'. For over ten years discussions have been held and projects designed aiming at the artificial expansion of the coast of the south-western part of Holland, the region were, among others, The Hague and Rotterdam are located, and that is densily populated and heavily industrialized. The project, as it gradually evolved, promises to provide space for 10.000 to 30.000 new housings and for extended recreational facilities. It will also bring about a major reinforcement of coast safety, a substantial extension of freshwater supply, the opportunity to implement alternative

13 The material I summarize here has been provided to me by Wim de Ridder, director of the Society and Enterprise Foundation (Stichting Maatschappij en Onderneming SMO), The Hague, The Netherlands

forms of energy and energy savings and a unique chance to develop new hydraulic technologies. It even promises to be cost-effective. This is enough, one would say, to generate wholehearted support from ministeries and national political parties. But years of concerted efforts by business and lower local agencies were needed to make authorities move, and they still think they are pushed irresponsibly. Recently, however, a public-private partnership has been established, and now the project seems well on its way.

In the socio-economic and socio-political environment of present-day Western societies, initiatives of such a participatory nature appear to be increasingly needed. Neither the market by itself, nor the state by itself is able to tackle adequately the problems facing us with regard to, say, the maintenance of decent welfare arrangements, or the growing threat of environmental disasters. Here joint initiatives are necessary, in the form of public-private partnerships, shifting alliances, often of a temporary nature, in which various constituencies recognize their shared interests in a common good and act accordingly. Such initiatives, in a sense, belong to the realm of **moral esthetics**: individuals, corporations and administrative agencies decide to participate in a joint project, not so much because it is the **right** thing to do, but because it is a **decent** thing to do.

What makes the Coast Location Plan interesting from a moral point of view is the fact that business could have found equal profits in a shorter time and in a less energy consuming way, and nevertheless chose to be persistent for about ten years. There is the fact that we witness here a peculiar process of **responsibility formation**. In a sense it is of secondary importance who first comes up with the idea for the project. It is the initiative that counts, more than the initiator. But once the project is sketched, however roughly, possible participants face the decision whether they will contribute, positively or negatively, to its realization. This way of getting involved in decision processes is characteristic of what has been called a **participatory democracy**[14]. It also gives birth to a specific type of ethics, which I indicate as **participatory ethics**. The basic principles of a participatory ethics are the principle of **decency** and the principle of **emancipation**. The principle of decency implies that where a real opportunity to contribute to the general welfare presents itself, one

14 See JANE MANSBRIDGE: *Beyond Adversary Democracy,* New York (Basic Books) 1980. Benjamin Barber speaks of 'strong democracy' as 'politics in the participatory mode', in his book: *Strong Democracy. Participatory Politics for a New Age*, Berkeley, Los Angeles, London (University of California Press) 1984, p. 150 seq.

should have solid moral reasons **not** to go for it. The principle of emancipation says that specific groups deserve the space and means for development that history has unwarrantedly denied them up to now.

Analysis of other-including actions under the moral viewpoint of common interests and roughly equal claims – or no claims at all – provides us with a fairly detailed picture of moral possibilities. These vary from simultaneous and connected interests, guided by a transactional ethics on the basis of the principles of equality, honesty and reciprocity, to shared interests, guided by a participatory ethics on the basis of the principles of decency and emancipation. But is this picture not too rosy? Are social relations in general, and market transactions especially, not, to a large extent, determined by **conflicting** instead of by common interests, and by striking **inequalities** of power, deafening the powerful with respect to whatever claim they can be confronted with?

There are two questions at stake here, one empirical and the other normative. The **empirical** question raises the issue whether, in market transactions notably, conflicting interests, inequality of power, and the subsequent – so the silent assumption goes – morally reproachable behavior are especially frequent. It is hard to tell, comparable data and objective criteria hardly being available. Of course, where money is involved, or where power is involved, and most certainly where both are involved, it is a calculated guess that irregularities will be abundant as well. As the theory of the facilitating circumstances teaches us: in the trade of second-hand cars, manners are likely to be less gentle than at the counter of the public library. But once the inviting circumstances are taken into account, it seems an equally calculated guess to assume that the distribution of saints and sinners in the market place is not strikingly different from that in politics, medicine or administration. The issue remains empirically undecidable, and therefore essentially contested.

The **normative** issue is of a different nature, for here the question no longer deals with **what is the case**, but with **what ought to be**, given the analytical possibility of an agent's action pattern being confronted with another person's conflicting interests and/or unevenly strong claims. It proves to be a real possibility, requiring solid moral thinking. For here, often, tough moral dilemmas arise.

c) Recognitional Ethics

We are facing a type of situation, in effect, that resembles the zero-sum game, in which the gain of the one equals the loss of the other, and the consolidated outcome is not a cooperative surplus, but zero. Notice that no doubts arise regarding the moral legitimacy of the various interests. The discussion is not about agents, negating or explicitly rejecting legitimate claims they could reasonably be expected to take into account, so the discussion is not about plain egoism and its obvious moral reproachability. Here all interests at stake are perfectly justified or at least justifiable from a moral point of view. They are only irreconcilable. Take the case of the plywood corporation that yearly imports a $350 million worth of hardwood from tropical forests in Indonesia, and that, by so doing, probably contributes to the greenhouse effect and most certainly to the destruction of the landscape, the extinction of plant and animal species, the destruction of cultural life and, often, of living conditions of indigenous people[15]. Here the interests at stake include those of the Indonesian government, trying to develop the country economically, next to the interests of the local population, of the timber corporation and of its consumers, as well as the interests of the world population, facing a gradual warming of the atmosphere with unforeseeable consequences, and the interests represented by individuals and groups trying to protect ecosystems for their own sake. Conflicting interests, no doubt, and differently powerful claims, to be acknowledged accordingly. The dilemma may not be insolvable, but the solution will require more than just a blindfold choice.

Similarly a corporation faces a serious moral question, in its hiring practices, when it is confronted with affirmative action and minority quotas as moral requirements. Unemployement of unskilled and semi-skilled workers of Surinamese descent living in Holland is three to four times higher than among native Dutch workers. The Surinamese unemployed mainly live in geographical areas where the unemployement rate is twice as high as the national average. The Dutch people, to some extent, have a historical debt to the people of Suriname, having once exploited them as the inhabitants of one of the Dutch colonies. Therefore, authorities and the Dutch population in general have recognized, at least implicitly, a certain moral compensatory duty towards people of Surinamese descent living in Holland. However, the national community is also well aware of the rights that unemployed native Dutch labourers

15 See LaRue Tone Hosmer: "Propical Plywood Imports, Inc.", Awarded Case in International Business Ethics, Alling foundation, Ethics in Business, Graduate School of Business, Columbia University.

may assert, as they are laid off abruptly, or obstructed in finding a first job in spite of serious and continuing efforts. In such a situation, whatever policy a corporation chooses, it necessarily will interfere in patterns of conflicting interests, based on strong claims, often presented as moral rights.

Cases of conflicting interests combined with strong moral claims are not only common in business relations. In the medical sphere, in administrative policies, in domestic and international politics and in various professional areas, conflicts of rights and interests arise quite regularly. Ethics, especially applied ethics, in the last decades has concentrated its efforts to a large extent on the clarification and handling of tough moral dilemmas in everyday life, with real results, one might say. In many professional circles the awareness has increased **that** moral issues are at stake, and many people don't shy away anymore from tackling them in a straightforward manner. What is required, in order to tackle the problems adequately, is the **recognition that** rights are involved, and the **skill** to bring about **morally legitimate trade-offs** between the different rights and interests at stake. It's not the morality of the market place we see at work here, with common interests and equal claims as binding agents. Here we witness the morality of the recognition of strong rights and conflicting interests. Once we develop this morality into a full-fledged ethical theory, we may get what I would call a **recognitional ethics**, next to the transactional and the participatory ethics I mentioned earlier. For many a practitioner, recognitional ethics constitutes the heart of his or her moral endeavours, for this type of ethics is about the real tough choices to be made.

We are talking about types of ethics derived from varieties of other-including actions. It may help to notice that the relation between the agent and others, included in the action pattern, is specific in each of the three types of ethics we distinguished up to now. Within the realm of transactional ethics, agent and others are related as abstract equals, each claiming a similar space of freedom for action, as a minimum condition in the case of simultaneous interests, and, in the case of connected interests, occasionally claiming from the other an amount of cooperation similar to that one is prepared to provide oneself in joint ventures for mutual benefits. Within the realm of participatory ethics, the relation between agents is characterised by voluntarily assumed solidarity in pursuit of a common good, in which, however, the participation of the other can be claimed by nobody. It is, in a sense, an occasional initiative taken by somebody that triggers the rise of non-enforceable obligations to which participants commit themselves. Within the realm of recognitional ethics, the relation between agents is characterized by **asymmetry**, one agent presenting herself as bearer of a strong claim, if not an explicit moral right, and so acting as **claimant**, and the other finding herself under the obligation to recognize the present claim, and so acting as **duty-bound** vis-à-vis the claimant. A corporation has made extensive investments to introduce a new product that, once available on the market, in spite of all precautions, seems to cause carcinogenic side effects. At the very moment the knowledge of a real risk presents itself, even before consumer organisations or governmental authorities get informed, the corporation faces the moral duty of stopping further production and recalling the product, potential users of the product acting, unknowingly, as one powerful collective claimant. It is clear that the positions of claimant and duty-bound can change according to the circumstances.

The principles of a recognitional ethics follow the asymmetry of the positions within it. Basic is the formal **principle of recognition** of well-founded claims and rights. Once we accept that, under given conditions, the asymmetrical situation may occur to a duty-bound subject, individual, group or organisation, facing a moral claimant, we have to accept also the moral obligation of the duty-bound agent to recognize the right or rights at stake. Next to this formal principle a more substantial principle is needed to guide specific actions. Here two possibilities present themselves. The first one is strongly rights-oriented. One tries to develop a well-ordered 'table of rights' together with some 'principle of priority', saying, for instance, that some rights are to be considered as 'basic' or '-fundamental', at least *prima facie*, or stating that, in cases of conflict, rights precede interests[16]. In present-day ethical theory the rights-oriented approach predominates. However, a second approach is possible. It makes use, at appropriate moments, of the concept of rights, but tries to encompass interests as well. As a result, it may prove better suited for action patterns in which, next to rights, interests play a significant role, and in situations in which no explicit claims are at stake. For example,

16 In his recent book *The Ethics of International Business*, Oxford (Oxford University Press) 1989, Thomas Donaldson presents a list of ten fundamental international rights, together with a 'fairness-affordability condition', as minimum moral requirements for corporations operating within international relations. And in his much-used book *Business Ethics. Concepts and Cases*, Englewood Cliffs (Prentice Hall) [2]1988, p. 116–118, MANUEL VELASQUEZ tentatively offers some rules-of-thumb for prioritizing between rights, justice and interests.

possible individual claimants may remain undetermined, but, nevertheless, certain moral rules obtain in view of the common good. It comes down, in effect, to a revivification of the old **principle of beneficence** in a more elaborated way.

In its unelaborated form the principle constitutes the basis of every moral rule, saying: 'Bonum faciendum et malum vitandum', as medieval philosophers stated, translating Aristotle into Latin. Translated once more: "The good should be done and the bad be avoided". To make the principle sound less lapidary, several suggestions for further articulation have been made. Among them the often quoted version William Frankena presents:

> What does the principle of beneficence say? Four things, I think:
> 1. One ought not to inflict evil or harm (what is bad).
> 2. One ought to prevent evil or harm.
> 3. One ought to remove evil.
> 4. One ought to do or promote good[17].

I for myself think that it makes sense to have the principle say six things:

1. Avoid doing harm
2. Repair or compensate the harm you did
3. Prevent harm being done by others
4. Avoid bringing about conditions that generate harm
5. Repair or compensate harm done by others
6. Do good wherever and whenever you can[18].

A sharp distinction is often made between the first three and the last three sub-principles. The former are considered as universally binding, whereas from the fourth sub-principle onward we would find ourselves in the realm of laudable but not obligatory actions. I am afraid this is too simple a conception of the spreading of moral responsibilities. It is quite possible that, in a given situation, the costs involved in preventing harm done by others are so high that preventive action can no longer be said to be a moral duty. One evening in the spring of 1982, three CBS technicians, Leo Kuranski, Robert Schulze, and Edward Benford, came upon Margaret Barbera being dragged by a man through an isolated parking garage along the Hudson River in Manhattan. Even though the assailant

17 W. FRANKENA: *Ethics*, Englewood Cliffs (Prentice Hall) ^{2}1973) p. 47.

18 In: "According to Local Circumstances. Teaching Business Ethics on Both Sides of the Atlantic", *Moral Education Forum*, 16 (Winter 1991), 4, p. 29 sq. I have commented the six sub-principles here presented.

was brandishing a long-barreled pistol, the three men rushed to Barbera's aid – into their death[19]. The men tried to prevent harm being done by another. But their behaviour, undoubtedly courageous and highly respectable, was far beyond the call of moral duty. It is also very conceivable that, in a different situation, the moral obligation to avoid bringing about conditions that generate harm are unconditional. Johnson and Johnson was highly applauded for its reaction in the Tylenol case, and rightly so. But had it acted in a less unconditional way, and had this reaction become known to the public, the corporation would have been charged with a general moral indignation, and equally rightly so. It can even be that, under specific circumstances, the moral obligation to contribute to the repair of harm done by others appears to be inescapable. During the last decades, in many industrialized countries water and soil pollution has reached extreme degrees. The costs of cleaning up the damage often are enormous, whereas the pollutors prove to be unidentifiable or untraceable. This, however, does not relieve the community from the moral obligation to make strenuous efforts, may they be extremely expensive, to restore the environment as far as possible, in view of its present inhabitants, and, even more so, in view of future generations. The advantage of using an articulated version of the principle of beneficence in approaching morally meaningful situations is precisely that it allows a great flexibility in the application of basic moral insights, enabling us to come very close to the specificities of the situation at stake. Once we accept that all six sub-principles deserve to be taken as **possible** moral guidelines, the actual spreading of responsibilities may be determined in an adequate way.

Pivotal within the realm of recognitional ethics is the **strength** of the claim presented, and the **good reasons** that are given for its moral **legitimacy**. Final arbiter in these matters is the moral community of well-informed, decent and impartial citizens, continuously assessing factual behavioral patterns and reasonable standards of human exchange. Recognitional ethics does not **make** agents behave more ethically, and neither do transactional nor participatory ethics. It specifies existing moral guidelines, and may help to generate new ones in cases where they have not yet been developed. But, in itself, it does not prevent the free rider and the crook from acting as they like. As I said earlier, self-directed actions can remain unchallenged. In that case they are only governed by

19 The story appears in ROBERT FRANK: *Passions Within Reason* (see note 10), pp. 44–45.

the moral principle of self-development. They also can be challenged in a morally legitimate way. The agent that recognizes the legitimacy of the challenge, by so doing leaves the realm of self-directed actions and enters the domain of other-including actions, governed by the various principles with which we have now become familiar. The manager considering the reorganization of a division, including possible lay-offs, may face legitimate claims by employees who, over the years, have acquired certain rights to be taken into account. Once the manager acknowledges these rights and makes them part of the decision process, the challenged self-directed action of reconstructing the firm becomes an other-including action, morally specified by conflicting interests and strong claims. We are, then, on firm recognitional grounds. However, if, for selfish reasons, the agent chooses to reject a legitimate claim, ethical theory is unable to stop him. Here only the moral community may be succesful, by using the various devices of enforcement at its disposal that range from public indignation via social exclusion to legal sanctions.

The taxonomy of ethical behavior on the basis of a typology of action patterns yields a fairly articulated scheme of moral principles, as Fig. 1 shows. It is worth noticing that, with regard to the 'morality of the market place', business ethics as a discipline up to now has confined itself largely to the domain of recognitional ethics. Subjects like moral rights in the workplace, stakeholder analysis, protection of the environment against industrial aggression, boundaries of marketing practices, whistle-blowing, and social investment, proliferate in the ever increasing number of textbooks and in the professional journals. This is not really surprising, for, of old, the domain of rights and correlative duties has been the privileged terrain of ethical exercises. Given the fact, however, that market transactions, to a large extent, are characterized by common interests in different degrees, and by roughly equal claims, and that the phenomenon of shifting alliances and temporary public-private partnerships in which business is involved are undoubtedly on the increase, it seems appropriate that the principles of transactional and of participatory ethics, too, should get the attention they deserve. It is my conviction that the contours of a participatory ethics, especially, need further elaboration, its principles being as uncommon as they are promising in the present state of affairs.

III. Ethics in a Participatory Market Society

1. The Rehabilitation of Civil Society

The idea of participatory social relations has mainly been developed in the context of **political** theory, more specifically as a specimen of a theory of democracy. Jane Mansbridge distinguishes an **adversary** and a **participatory** democracy[20], and Benjamin Barber speaks of a 'strong democracy in the participatory mode'[21]. He offers the following formal definition:

> Strong democracy in the participatory mode resolves conflict (...) through a participatory process of ongoing, proximate self-legislation and the creation of a political community capable of transforming dependent private individuals into free citizens and partial and private interests into public goods[22].

He develops the definition by stating:

> Participatory politics deals with public disputes and conflicts of interests by subjecting them to a never-ending process of deliberation, decision, and action. (...) Strong democracy relies on participation in an evolving problem-solving community that creates public ends where there were none before (...). In such communities, public ends (...) are literally forged through the act of public participation, created through common deliberation and common action and the effect that deliberation and action have on interests, which change shape and direction when subjected to these participatory processes[23].

As often in political theory, the starting point is formed by **conflicting** interests and public **dispute**, but the emphasis in participatory politics is on the problem-solving **community** that creates public ends where there were none before.

It should be noted, however, that participatory ethics is not a prerogative of what can be called, strictly speaking, **communities**, in the communitarian, almost ontological sense of clearly circumscribed social entities, enjoying an unchallenged cohesion linked to lasting and unconditional commitments of its members. Participatory arrangements are rather of the nature of temporary 'we-alliances', originating from prag-

20 See *Beyond Adversary Democracy.*

21 See Jane Mansbridge: *Strong Democracy. Participatory Politics in a New Age.*

22 *Ibid.*, p. 151.

23 *Ibid.*, pp. 151–152.

matic opportunities and equally pragmatic initiatives, aimed at limited but clearly defined objectives, often in the sphere of public goods, or, more generally, the common good.

But why do people engage in such activities? What motives do they have to accept constraints on their pursuit of interests, and to contribute to public ends? Mixed motives, quite probably. But among these motives might be what the eighteenth century's philosopher David Hume describes as duties undertaken "from a sense of obligation when we consider the necessities of human society"[24]. Hume links this sense of obligation to the **experience of mutual dependence**. This experience has kept growing incesssantly since the late eighteenth and early nineteenth century. Today more than ever we acknowledge that, no doubt, our freedom has increased, but so has our interdependence. We acknowledge that, to a large extent, we have to use our extended decision making powers to handle our dependencies. And this acknowledgement may well be at the origin of people's willingness to engage in cooperative ventures in view of public ends.

The same idea of the constructive acknowledgement of mutual dependence can also be approached in another way. It has long been thought that, to regulate social order, modern people basically have only two devices at their disposal, the market and the state. The market as the self-regulating mechanism for the pursuit of self-interest, the state as the authoritative regulatory mechanism where the market fails. Yet, from the beginning of modern times, an alternative has been present to both the market and the state, namely **civil society**, understood as the realm where people recognize "the gift of society", the realm of potentially creative interdependencies, the domain in which people as free citizens cooperate to determine their common destiny by initiating real-life projects, nearby as well as future-oriented. Civil society is the social sphere in which people recognize that autonomy includes responsibilities. The idea of a 'civil society' has long been hidden by the alleged supremacy of market arrangements and state interventions as regulatory forces in social life. Today civil society once again attracts the attention of sociologists and political theorists. As Alan Wolfe puts it:

> We learn how to act toward others because civil society brings us in contact with people in such a way that we are forced to recog-

24 Quoted in ALAN WOLFE: *Whose Keeper? Social Science and Moral Obligation*, Berkeley, Los Angeles, London (University of California Press) 1989, p. 15.

> nize our dependence on them. We ourselves have to take responsibility for our moral obligations, and we do so through this gift called society that we make for ourselves. What makes us modern, in short, is that we are capable of acting as our own moral agents. If modernity means a withering away of such institutions as the tight-knit family and the local community that once taught the moral rules of interdependence, modern people must simply work harder to find such rules for themselves[25].

The rehabilitation of civil society implies a strong emphasis on moral obligations of a totally new kind. Earlier I called them **non-enforceable obligations**. Given the mutual dependence that binds **and** supports all participants in modern society, they morally can be expected to **retribute by contributing** to the common good. In that sense there is a **general** obligation on everybody. However, the obligation not being specified, it neither can be enforced. To become effective, autonomous adults are needed who recognize that, individually and collectively, they themselves have to take responsibility for the common good.

It is an odd kind of obligation that is at stake here, not imposed but voluntarily accepted. Today it is desperately needed nonetheless. A growing number of important social projects can only be brought about by voluntary cooperation of various parties, business, government, administrative officials, interest groups and the media. Environmental policies can no longer exclusively be imposed from above, the shaping of decent welfare arrangements can not be left solely to the government and to political parties. Civil society expects various participants to take their share of responsibility at various occasions. That is the price we pay for coming of age in an era of full-fledged autonomy embedded in irreversible interdependence.

'Civil society' as it is used here is a plainly **normative** concept with unmistakable moral undertones. As such, it describes more what ought to be than what is the case. Normative concepts of such a broad and evocative nature often appear to be fixed to the rainbow, a bright but very unstable fixing point indeed. The justification for giving it a central place nevertheless comes from the observation that, increasingly, **opportunities** for the implementation of civil society as a texture of shifting alliances present themselves in present-day developed societies.

Participatory ethics is the ethics of civil society. It does not replace the morality of the market place, nor does it render superfluous the moral

25 *Ibid.*, pp. 19; 14–19.

ity that acknowledges legitimate claims where it sees them. It rather complements both. Participatory ethics, the ethics of non-enforceable obligations, accompanies the emergence of new moral opportunities and social initiatives considered utopian before. Recognitional ethics makes us accept the rights and claims that individuals and groups have acquired in the past. Transactional ethics makes us cooperate for mutual benefit in the present. Participatory ethics helps us look to our common future.

At the beginning I mentioned three ongoing discussions in social ethics to which my argument is related, more or less directly: the discussion about motives and intentions with regard to self-interest, the discussion about egoism and altruism as basic concepts in social ethics, and the discussion about prudence and morality, especially in the market place. We have largely eliminated motives, and emphasized intentions instead. We have discovered egoism and altruism as moral extremes, with the interesting and challenging varieties of ethical behaviour being located between them. But we have referred to the apparent dichotomy between prudence and morality only very indirectly. It was not needed for the construction of our argument. Sometimes a dichotomy gently disappears, simply due to the appearance on the scene of a more articulated model. If the taxonomy of various ethical behaviours has this effect on the prudence – morality dichotomy, we will have achieved an unintended additional gain. The whithering away, on the theoretical level, of a traditional dichotomy, may help to open the door to practices in which corporations willingly accept specific civil responsibilities, not primarily for profit reasons, but neither refusing the concomitant benefits that may accompany their choices. In a participatory market society, civil corporations are almost human.

TAXONOMY OF ETHICAL BEHAVIOUR

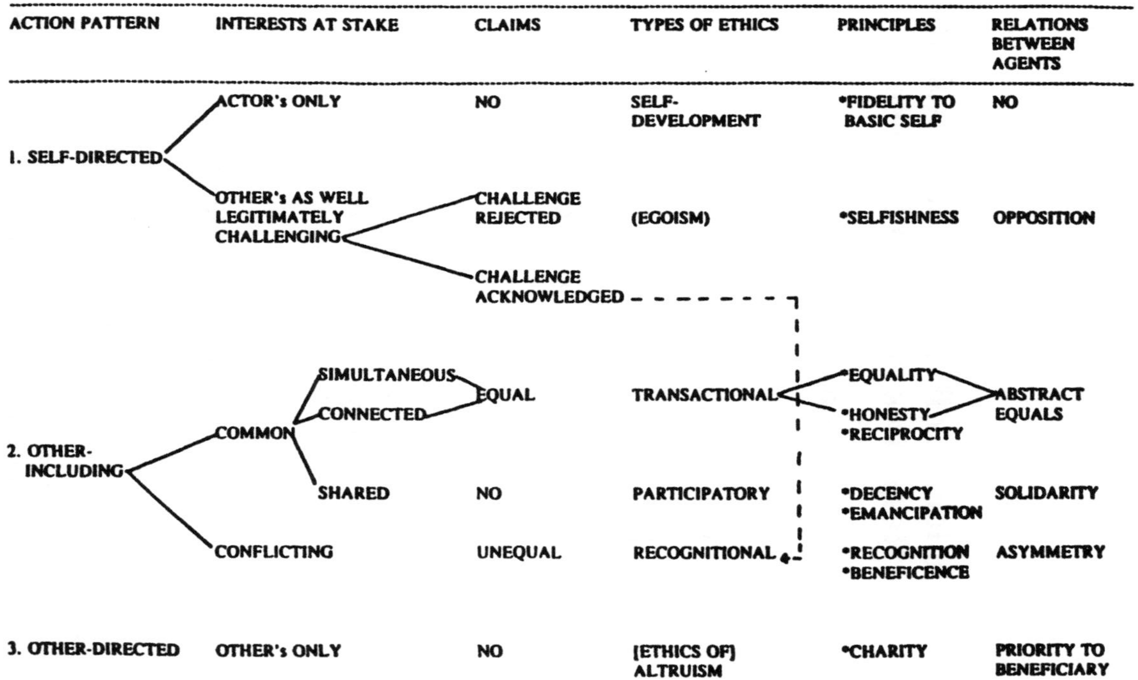

Chapter 2

Upholding or Breaking Ethical Rules? – Responses to Ethical Problems

VERNER C. PETERSEN

How is it possible to ensure at the same time that one is bound by rules that protect one from irrational or unethical behaviour—and that these rules do not turn into prisons from which it is not possible to break out even when it would be rational to do so? (ELSTER, 1989b, p. 120)

I. Another Ethical Dilemma

A common theme of the recent deluge of books and articles on ethics, and especially business ethics, seems to be the need for ethical rules. Rules like the ones found in the so-called ethical codes of a firm. Every firm its own ethical code.

In general, there also seem to be agreement on what constitutes the most relevant ethical issues, like the concern for the environment in various forms, from whales and dolphins to the ozone layer, or the interests of the stakeholders as expressed in a business manifesto for the Rio Earth Summit: "we must expand our concept of those who have a stake in our operations to include not only employees and shareholders but also suppliers, neighbours, citizens' groups and others"[1].

1 *The Guardian*, Friday, May 8, 1992.

UPHOLDING OR BREAKING ETHICAL RULES?

A quick look at the way the different issues are treated leads to the impression that a kind of tacit agreement on what constitutes good and bad business practices is taken for granted.

The only real dilemma left open for discussion seems to be the conflict between the economic considerations and the ethical considerations. "There is a 'right' or 'proper' or 'just' balance between economic performance and social performance, and the dilemma of management comes in finding it."[2]

According to this view, existing ethical rules are taken for granted with a certain smugness. There is almost no discussion of how ethical rules are created, broken and changed. No discussion of how and why they are followed or enforced. No discussion of who decides what is right or wrong. No discussion of the possible relation between power and ethics. Ethical rules are ethical and that is more or less that.

Underneath all that another ethical dilemma lies hidden. The dilemma Elster is talking about[3]. Ethical rules may have been erected to protect us against certain forms of behaviour that might be detrimental, but the same rules can turn into the bars of a prison preventing behaviour that might be beneficial.

This paper takes up some of these issues and opens up for a discussion of the self-satisfied and conflict-free view of ethics. In a way it is an attempt to blow away some of the existing ethical cobwebs of the mind. In order to do so, the paper investigates how we respond to ethical problems. How we use ethical rules, if we use them, how we try to uphold rules or alternatively how we try to change rules, and finally the role of power and the will-to-power in our responses.

Books on business ethics often contain short introductory chapters on what constitutes an ethical decision. As a rule one may choose between some kind of utilitarianism, act- or rule utilitarianism, and a version of duty or obligation related to a Kantian version of ethics.[4]

In the first instance the response to an ethical problem is decided by an appeal to the utility of the solutions. One has to choose the decision that leads to the greatest utility for the greatest number, to paraphrase Bentham[5]. In a modern form this view can be found in Buchanan[6].

2 HOSMER (1991).
3 ELSTER (1989b).
4 DONALDSON (1990).
5 BENTHAM (1789).
6 BUCHANAN (1985).

In the other instance one has to appeal to one's duty, obligation or simply to what is considered right or fair. This view is related to Kant's categorical imperative: "Act only according to that maxim whereby you can at the same time will that it should become a universal law"[7]. Added to that is the idea that other people ought to be treated as ends in themselves and not as means to the furthering of one's own goals.

What is usually forgotten is that power may play an important role in deciding ethical problems and in determining what is seen as ethical. Power is exercized when one person forces another person to do something the other person would not otherwise have done, or when one person decides the agenda for other people.[8] In this way those in power may uphold their version of ethical rules and rule-following behaviour. Such a system of power also lies behind every attempt to uphold rules through control and sanctions.

A kind of will-to-power may be found in the power to break rules, the power to disregard rules, the power to destroy an existing fabric of rules. Perhaps it is possible to distinguish between power to uphold an existing set of rules and power to break existing rules. Using will-to-power as an expression of the latter kind is inspired by Nietzsche's use of this term. Of will-to-power he wrote: "er wird wachsen, um sich greifen, an sich ziehen, Übergewicht gewinnen wollen, – nicht aus irgendeiner Moralität oder Immoralität heraus, sondern weil er *lebt*, und weil Leben eben Wille zur Macht ist"[9].

This may be related to the kind of power Machiavelli talked about when he asserted: "... experience in our time shows that those princes have done great things who have valued their promises little, and who have understood how to addle the brains of men with trickery; and in the end they have vanquished those who have stood upon their honesty"[10].

In more recent times Carr tells us that business men at some time or other behave like Machiavellian princes in order to further their business.[11]

Seen from the perspective representing the will-to-power, existing ethical rules may be seen as fetters on new thoughts, new decisions and new actions. Fetters that have to be broken in an attempt to acquire another vision of the world.

---

7 KANT (1785), p. 30.
8 LUKES (1974).
9 NIETZSCHE (1886), p. 153.
10 MACHIAVELLI (1513), p. 106.
11 CARR (1968).

The paper asserts that the response to ethical problems is influenced by a combination of the way other people act, of control and sanctions, of appeals to duty and utility and finally of power and will-to-power. In this paper an attempt is made to group and analyze our responses to ethical problems. The following response-combinations were found interesting:

- The control and sanctions response
- The imitative adjustment response
- The pragmatic or cyclical-undetermined response
- The static trying-to-uphold response
- The dynamic trying-to-change response
- The bestial power response

In the final part of the paper these combinations are grouped according to whether they contribute to the upholding of certain rules or whether they contribute to the breaking of rules and the creation of new rules. In this way it is hoped that some light can be shed on Elster's dilemma.

II. Ethical Problems

By ethical problems we mean problems to which the possible solutions can loosely be characterized as being good or evil or somewhere in between, just or unjust or somewhere in between, right or wrong or somewhere in between. All according to what one personally feels is the case. It is not necessary that one should be able to state precisely why one feels the solution is good or bad or whatever.

It does not even have to be problems in which one is personally involved. Or problems where one feels well-informed. On the other hand, only problems where one's opinion or judgment matters in some way are relevant to our discussion. Other types of problems are not relevant. A technical problem, where one would have to form an opinion as to whether a certain technical solution would work or not is not an ethical problem.

Whether one is aware of the ethical content of the problem or not does not seem to be important. Many of our day-to-day ethical decisions are presumably made without thinking about them as ethical decisions. The important thing is that one should be able to give an ethically related reason for one's response when asked to do so.

What we are looking for are responses to ethical problems. Responses used to defend one's own position with regard to the different solutions in the form of decisions made, or actions undertaken, whether by one self or by others, in relation to the ethical problem.

III. The Control and Sanctions Response

When someone is asked why he was speeding, a common reply might be: "Well, I got there a little faster, and I judged the chance of being caught to be slight, and even if there had been a radar trap it would only have cost me 400 kroner or so...".

In this instance it seems that a rule concerning speed limits is violated because the risk of being caught breaking it is slight and the fine one would have to pay, if caught, considered insignificant. In this way the balance between one's own utility and the rule against speeding tipped in favour of one's self-interest.

In another situation a manager of a recycling firm might one day be told that the firm has a problem, because a container has developed a leak, and that 1000 litres of a dangerous liquid have been spilled. He has to decide what should be done. According to environmental ethical standards such spills should be contained, sucked up, and transported to a treatment plant. On the other hand it would be a lot cheaper just to hose it out through the drains.

In this case the manager decides that the spill should be contained and sent to the treatment plant. When asked why he decided to react in this way, he replies: "If we had decided just to hose it down the drains, the chances of being caught would have been high, as a lot of people would have known about it, and they would talk, ... and I know that the fines would have been very heavy, and so...".

His response matches the former response to the speeding question. It is based on the same simple rational calculation using the subjective calculated risk of being caught, "multiplied" by the heaviness of the fines and compared with what could be saved or gained by violating the rules.

In the former case the calculation led to the result that the rule was violated. In the other case the response was to follow the rule. This difference in outcome was not a result of any appeal to ethical principles. In principle the different decisions did not have anything to do with different ethical standards. It could be the same person, using the same kind of calculation in both instances.

Although these responses did not represent very ethical decisions, they may nevertheless be representative of the way most of us respond when faced with ethical dilemmas involving our own utility. Questions of one's duty or what might be in the interest of society do not enter into this type of response. Only the question of the subjectively calculated probability of being caught and the sanctions imposed on one if that should happen. Presumably the responses represent a rational weighing up of the risk times the severity of the sanctions, against the gain in utility that would be the result of violating the ethical rule.

The response to ethical problems in these instances can be seen as a result of the degree of supervision, control and the subjectively judged heaviness of the sanctions imposed on those caught breaking the rule. With this kind of response, ethical rules going against our self-interest would only be obeyed if there is a certain amount of supervision and control, and/or the sanctions for breaking the rules are harsh enough. This means that some kind of power apparatus exists, taking care of supervision, control and the metering out of sanctions.

Whether we were talking about the whole of society or just a single company, we would have to weigh the cost of expanding the apparatus of control and sanctions against the cost associated with the violations of rules, or the benefits associated with a widespread rule-following. The relation between costs and benefits might be as illustrated in figure 2:1. This figure is based on a figure found in Elster[12].

In a given organization, the net benefit of introducing control and sanctions to assure rule-following might be negative, because a small amount of control and some sanctions give rise to certain costs, without resulting in any noticeable increase in rule-following behaviour. The risk of being caught and the severity of the sanctions may be insignificant. Increasing the amount of control and making sanctions more severe will lead to a situation in which the benefit of control and sanctions become positive, and more control and heavier sanctions may result in a greater net benefit. Eventually, the costs of control and sanctions will outweigh the benefits, and net benefit will decline.

12 Elster (1989a).

Figure 2:1

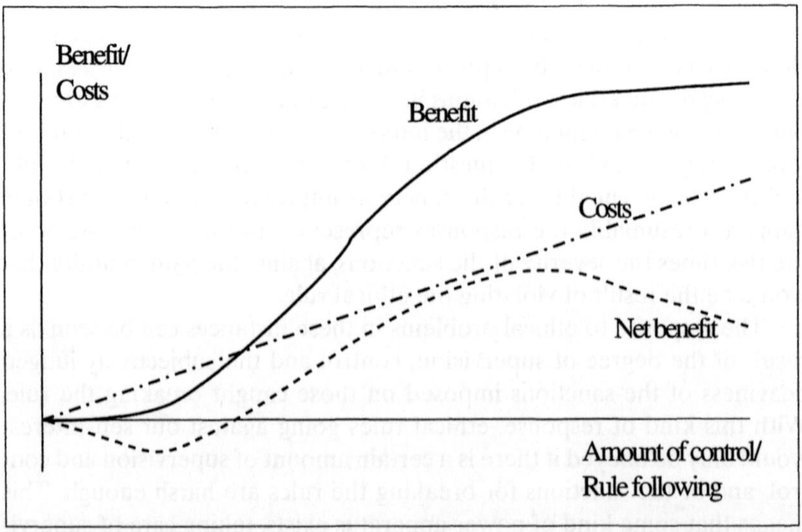

In a way this figure represents part of a dilemma that has become more important in most western societies and, presumably, in many private companies, too. The problem is compounded by the growing complexity of the rules, which makes it almost impossible to get enough supervision and control to make sure the rules are followed. This seems to be exactly what is happening in connection with schemes for tax evasion and fraudulent behaviour. The number and subtlety of the rules is increased, but the degree of supervision and control necessary to assure behaviour in accordance with the rules is prohibitive, and nobody wants it.

This means that if supervision, control and sanctions were the only way to make sure that ethical rules were followed, the cost of enforcing these rules would easily become prohibitive, and as a result supervision and control would become insufficient. The risk of being caught violating a rule would diminish and rule-breaking might become the order of the day. Unless other types of responses to ethical problems get us out of the dilemma that control and sanctions land us in.

IV. The Imitative Social Adjustment Response

"Why I try to avoid paying taxes by engaging in this tax evasion scheme? Because I can save money. ... Everybody I know uses some scheme or other to diminish the tax burden, so why shouldn't I? It seems to be the way everyone is behaving, so although I had some doubts in the beginning, it now seems perfectly OK to me".

What happens here is that schemes for tax evasion are spreading by some kind of imitation. Maybe this mechanism could also explain why people litter the streets. Everyone just sort of loses their litter in a not too offensive way, and maybe each and every one would feel slightly embarrassed if they actually went out of the way just to search for a rubbish bin.

This might explain all sorts of ethically problematic behaviour, brought about by people and companies adjusting to what is generally seen as a socially acceptable response. Such a mechanism could explain how spirals of bad behaviour can spread in a society without anyone feeling any guilt or a sense of something unethical being done. Ethical rules would in this instance be broken by people, who only did what their neighbours, friends and other people could be observed doing. Sometimes it might expected there would be slight twinges of doubt if the new response goes against some old rule-following behaviour, but this doubt would soon be left behind, in order to conform with other peoples' responses.

This means that people responding to ethical problems in this way would not always be able to state any deeper reasons for their behaviour. "I am just doing what everyone else is doing, and I haven't thought about the reasons for doing that, it just seems perfectly acceptable to me".

There would of course be a difference between the early adopters, who might have thought of some kind of deeper reason for doing as they do, maximizing self-interest or whatever, and the late adopters who just follow the simple rule, that what almost everyone else is doing cannot be all wrong, and even if it was in some way or other, it would not really matter, because they would feel stupid and isolated, if they did not do what everyone else is doing in these situations. This kind of thinking has led to the argument that what everyone does, ought to be seen as acceptable and so the rules should be changed accordingly. I wonder, where this kind of argument may lead.

Nobody can really see through all the difficult second- and third-order effects of their doing something. To take such effects into account would simply be impossible. But these second- and third-order effects would be there all the same. Thus one's own rule-violating behaviour might lead to changes in the behaviour of other people that sooner or later lead to further changes in one's own behaviour and so on in a sort of expanding bad spiral of rule-violating behaviour[13]. Another effect might be that breaking some rules might also lead to the violation of further rules.

On the other hand, the same mechanism could also explain how ethical rule-following behaviour might spread in a company or in society. Maybe rule-following behaviour could be expected to spread like some fashion trend. This might help explain the spreading of messages far removed from everyday experiences, such as "Save the fin whales", or "Save the tropical rain forest". Or, in a more important example, in the growing consideration for the environment in everyday decisions. In this way imitative behaviour might presumably lead to good spirals of rule-following behaviour.

This type of imitative response might be the single most important mechanism determining the way people behave with respect to ethical rules. Imitative socially adaptive behaviour can lead to bad spirals of rule-breaking behaviour as well as good spirals of rule-following behaviour. The responses are, so to speak, ethically neutral. The important point, though, is that this kind of behaviour is not the result of some conscious ethical decision by the individual, except for the decision not to stray too far from the way other people react to ethical issues.

How then does one make conscious ethical decisions with regard to ethical dilemmas? Some answers to this question may be found in the following response types.

V. The Pragmatic or Cyclical-undetermined Response

An employee, having recently discovered that the company he is employed by is engaged in some very dubious practices, is asked what he

13 AXELROD (1984).

is going to do, and the answer is: "I expect it would have been my duty to protest against these practices, and as far as I can see what happens is rather dangerous for the environment in the long run, but my attempts to talk about it have convinced me that the only result of a protest would be that I would be sacked and blacklisted, that's why I feel powerless, and so nothing will happen until somebody else does something"

This type of response could be seen as the response resulting from a conscious weighing-up of different ethical instances of appeal. It might be seen as a response in which one attempts to give an ethical judgment using considerations related to utility, to duty and to power, trying to strike the balance between them. Normally one would not carry out this process of weighing-up the different considerations, but when asked one would be able to provide a more or less coherent reasoning using these considerations.

The different considerations might be seen as forces determining a resultant, the actual response, as shown in figure 2:2.

Figure 2:2

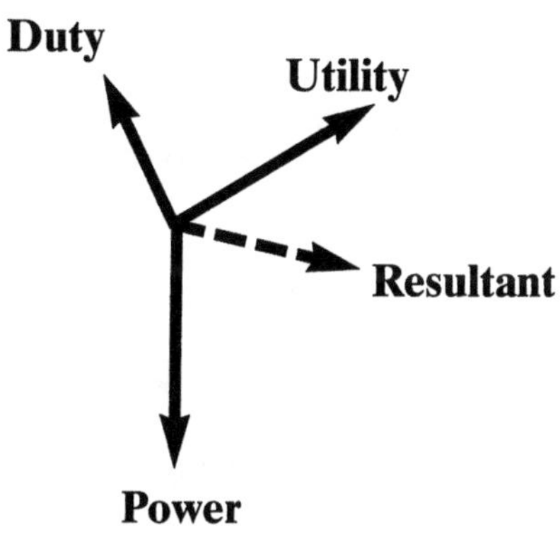

We can see how this might work by using an example. In this example a company, ARMLIMO plc, is producing a whole range of pesticides, using a process that threatens the immediate environment with dangerous pollutants, and the workers and people using the pesticides with long-term effects. On the other hand, using the pesticides definitely raises crop yield, and the company generates employment and income.

All the same, a group of radical environmentalists threatens to act against the company, through media happenings, boycott actions, and sabotage.

When people are asked how they judge the different threats, they often accept the boycott and media happenings, but balk at the sabotage to production and attempts to burn the plant. When asked for their reasoning, they answer somewhat like this: "Well, we must obey the law, and there is no law against production of the pesticides, and we also have to think about the consequences of stopping the production, the utility of the pesticides, and then, of course, the company has said that it would move the production to India if somebody attempted to hinder the production. I accept that the stuff might be dangerous, so something should be done, but sabotage, definitely no".

This rational approach to an ethical problem takes into account a lot of different considerations. It seems open and tolerant. But it does not actively judge the problem ethically. The resulting balance can be seen as just a passive adaptation to existing forces that one does not want to disturb. All forces are taken into account. The only thing that does not count is one's own opinion. This view does not initiate action or change. Instead, it pragmatically adapts to surrounding forces.

Figure 2:3

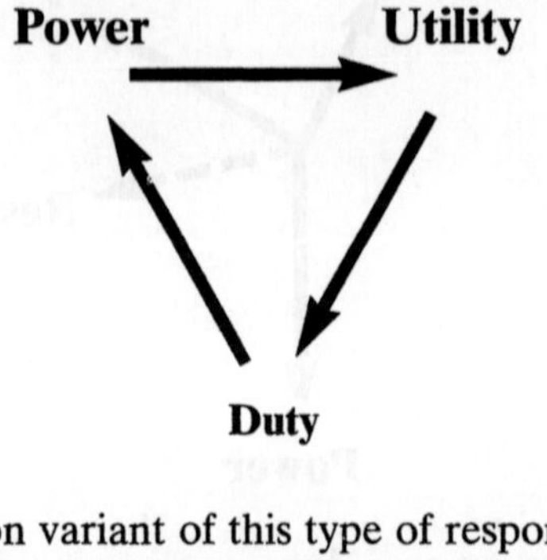

A not uncommon variant of this type of response might be to cycle through a cyclical triad. Changing viewpoint according to the views of the people around one or according to the depth of questioning. Cycling from a power view, "they say (the company, or the environmental groups) that if ..., and so...", to a utilitarian view, "it generates a lot of income, doesn't it, and so...", to a duty view, "we have a duty to close down this kind of production", and finally back to a power view. This response is represented in figure 2:3. Here one simply chooses the first appeal that comes to mind, until someone says: "but you haven't considered this and this". After this one cycles to another position.

VI. The Static Trying-to-uphold Response

The situation is the same as before. An employee has discovered some very dubious practices used by the company he is employed by. Again he is asked, but this time his answer is: "I have already protested to the manager, but he only tried to threaten me. He did not succeed, I intend to complain about these unethical practices anyway, and leave the company if nothing comes of it. To do anything else would simply be unethical".

This is a response which appeals to duty, to given ethical rules, to the law as it is. Or it might be a response which more or less directly appeals to utility considerations, of either the act- or the rule utility variant.

In the first instance rules may be of the Ten Commandments type: Thou shall not kill, lie, or commit adultery. In other words rules providing barriers against certain kinds of behaviour, and rules telling how to behave under certain conditions. A kind of social traffic rules telling us what to do and what not under all sorts of circumstances.

Many of the rules are related to the religious sphere, presumably upholding certain beliefs, and ideas of what is good and what is evil. The working of this kind of rules can be seen in the heated debates and actions for and against abortion and birth control, or the workings of a moral majority.

Other rules are more or less directly related to upholding a given social order, a given society, or simply the state in totalitarian regimes. In a democratic state these rules may define what actions are to be regarded as being democratic, and what not. More specifically they may define which types of decision-making procedures for solving social problems are ethical and which are not.

Rules of this type are also found in companies, sometimes under the name of ethical code, or, as IBM calls it, Business Conduct Guidelines, specifying explicitly what to do when dealing with the colleagues, with customers, with other companies, or in protecting the environment. Rules like these may also define loyal behaviour of an employee towards the firm.

Utility rules may seem quite different from these types of rules. But at least the non-religious rules may in fact be based on, or closely related to, utility considerations. The general argument may run like this: It is in the interest of all members of society that this rule exists. Or in the case of a company code, like this: obeying these rules will make the company more profitable in the long run. This seems to represent a significant part of the aim of business conduct guidelines.

It should perhaps be noted that these rules need not all be found in a written form. They can pervade a society or a company without even being mentioned because they may consist of certain habits, or ways of doing things without discussing them.

The important thing about these rules is that the beast is being tamed, and provided with an ethical collar. The beast being tamed is, of course, human nature, or even the will-to-power as shown in figure 2:4. "Jede moral ist, im Gegensatz zum laisser aller, ein Stück Tyrannei gegen die 'Natur' ... "[14].

Talking about an ethical collar is just a way of expressing that this kind of rules always seems to be tailor-made to uphold certain conditions or relations. And that may mean they function most efficiently when they are taken for granted and used as barriers to behaviour that one does not talk about, or even think about. The more important of these rules should preferably be seen as unchangeable, as something that is relevant under all conditions. This is part of their static nature, and it cannot be in any other way. If they were seen as relative, as dependent on time and circumstances, they might be open to change and interpretations, and they would loose some of their ability to support a certain order of things.

We are inclined to judge a response as being ethical if it is made according to such rules, and it is all the more ethical the more it is seen as response uninfluenced by other considerations, like the arm-twisting or other forms of power-induced behaviour. If it is made only under the threat of sanctions or under other forms of duress, it is not to be regarded as an ethical response. It is instead a response of the control and sanctions type.

There may be some doubt whether this is always so. Disapproval by others may represent some kind of sanction not based on power, but still inducing one to follow ethical rules. This may even be the way one learns of and adapts to ethical rules as ethical rules, seldom actually knowing the reason for them. Somewhat like learning a language without learning the rules of grammar[15]. This does seem to be in accord with the way ethical rules function. It should be noted that this mechanism is of the same type as the mechanism found in connection with imitative behaviour. The difference being that here one actually learns that the rules are ethical.

---

14 NIETZSCHE (1886), p. 78.

15 BODEN (1990).

Figure 2:4

Attempts to make the collar tighter-fitting may result in responses of an increasingly moralizing nature. And maybe Nietzsche touches one of the weak spots in this kind of moral system when he declares: "alles, was den einzelnen über die Herde hinaushebt und dem Nächsten Furcht macht, heißt von nun an *böse*; die billige, bescheidene, sich einordnende, gleichsetzende Gesinnung, das *Mittelmaß* der Begierden kommt zu moralischen Namen und Ehren"[16].

Maybe this is why most of us, when we observe people trying to act according to all the different kinds of rules falling in this category, tend to think: "They are slightly stupid, aren't they? They may be good, but somewhat limited in their mental capabilities". If they actively promote rule-following behaviour they may seem not only stupid, but even a bit dangerous. Incredulously we then ask ourselves: "They cannot mean that, can they?".

Sometimes one might go even further and say: "This isn't right, those damned rules must be destroyed". And then try to fight them in almost every way possible. This represents an attempt to change existing rules and values in some conscious way.

VII. The Dynamic Trying-to-change Response

A group of radical environmentalists sabotages the production of pesticides at the ARMLIMO company by burning down part of the plant, in

16 NIETZSCHE (1886), p. 90.

an attempt to stop the pollution from the plant and the production of dangerous pesticides. After being caught and imprisoned, they are asked for their reasons and their answer is: "We protested for a long time, but nothing happened because most people evidently thought that the benefit of having this large company generate employment and income far outweighed ethical aspects. Then we decided to use every means possible to stop the production, breaking some ethical rules for the sake of something we believe more important. Yes, force was used, and it demanded a lot of will-power".

In this case some of the ethical rules of our civil society were broken, using force, and appealing to another set of ethical reasons. And is that not a common phenomenon when the existing values of a society are being changed? Established rules are violated and have to be violated in order to promote new values. This happens when terrorists condemned for their violations of fundamental ethical rules in a society turn into freedom fighters or founding fathers of a new society. It may happen when dissidents of certain regimes try to overthrow the regimes using means that may seem unethical to the existing order. If they succeed their values become the new values and old values are destroyed.

It does not have to be all that dramatic. In everyday situations one may experience some kind of conflict that leads to conscious violations of ethical rules. It may happen because rules in certain situations are in conflict, forcing one to choose one rule and violate other rules. It may happen because research has shown that our present behaviour might become a liability in the long run. It may happen because new scientific and technical developments have led to new possibilities. Exemplified by the possibilities in medicine and in genetic engineering. Or it may happen because unquestioned social development has led to conditions under which new groups of people demand changes in existing values. It does not have to be part of any big scheme for change. It can be small scale rule-violations serving some goal felt to be more important, without actually thinking through the possible consequences. This means that the results can be contra-intuitive, leading to decisions and behaviour no one wanted.

People acting in these situations try to change an existing order through their will-to-power, breaking through the old established barriers to behaviour, representing common good and duties, the reasons for which have long been forgotten. Figure 2:5 attempts to illustrate this breaking through existing barriers.

People acting in this way go against the people in power, protected by exactly those rules and by supervision, control and sanctions. They may even make those using the imitative socially-acceptable response aware of what they are doing, forcing them to think about the reasons for their behaviour, thereby promoting changes even in their behaviour.

All this of course is related to questions of disobedience; after all rule-breaking is a kind of disobedience. But is that not the same thing as the rule-violations seen in connection with the control and sanctions response? I am not sure of the answer, but it seems that the kind of rule-violation related to civil obedience, represents something else. Although we cannot know for sure, we would expect everyone practicing civil disobedience to do so mostly in disregard of personal interests, in total contrast to what was the case, when people violated rules because they would gain by doing so, or just because everyone else did. This is at least evident in situations where people violating the rules pay a personal penalty for doing so.

Figure 2:5

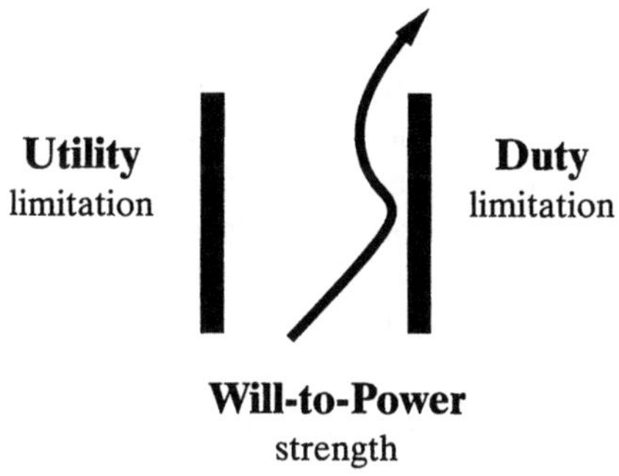

There is a dilemma in all this, though. How can one decide whether rule violations represent attempts to make beneficial changes to society or to the organization one belongs to? What is the difference between "good" and "evil" violations, so to speak? This is a very difficult question to answer in practice, although we are answering it all the time. The size of the penalty that people are willing to pay does not in itself indicate that what they are trying to do or to promote is more right, or better, than what they are opposed to or disobedient of.

Sometimes one may not even be given the possibility of expressing an answer. Power has already decided the issue, and one may have to accept the new order, hiding any doubt about the change. Or live with the old rules without feeling strong enough to express one's agreement with attempts to change them. This, however, is not the issue here. What we want to know is how one can answer the question without being forced to accept one answer.

One way might be to avoid taking a standpoint altogether by saying. "I do not think it concerns me, it might in the long run, but somehow the right answer will be evident by then".

A second way might represent the next step. Instead of trying to ignore the question, one observes how other people react to the violations and the reasons given for them. This might be a mechanism used by most people, but it certainly leads back to the imitative socially adaptive behaviour. Which means that one ignores the question, letting others decide. Forgetting that one's imitative response helps decide the issue, but in a way that one is not really aware of.

A third way of judging the rule-violations might be to look for possible motives. Rule-violations motivated by self-interest alone, without benefit to society, would then be condemned. The problem is that it might be difficult to gain insight into the real motivations. They might be hidden behind rhetoric or discredited by people having opposite interests.

A fourth way might be to look into the relations between what is happening in one area, and changes other areas one is not usually aware of. In this instance, change is accepted if it fits into other changes seen as positive, in whatever way that is being decided.

A fifth way might be to look into the relations between what is happening and some deeply-founded ethical rules, hardly realized until this moment. In this instance change is accepted if one realizes, or is being persuaded to realize, that it is in accord with some deeply felt, and not easily altered values. Acceptance may be almost immediate, if one has personally experienced the dilemma that the proposed change promises to solve, as a certain uneasiness with the existing order of things. Then rule-violations by a small number of individuals may induce immediate changes even in big organizations or societies. This may help us understand how big changes can sweep through society within a short span of time. Almost in the same way that a slight disturbance to a glass of undercooled water induces an immediate phase change, meaning of course that the water turns into a solid lump of ice.

Still, these reactions, whether they accept the new values or not, cannot ensure that the result is beneficial or even "better". It may become a gigantic social trial-and-error experiment, which has to be called off at some later stage because of the results it brought about. Called off, that is by the same kind of will-to-power actions that brought it about. Is that not in a way what happens when totalitarian regimes break down, or when socialist societies dissolve into semi-chaos?

The same goes for organizations, although Howell and Avolio[17] try to show how one can discern an unethical charismatic leader from an ethical. Their differentiation is based on discerning characteristics like, "uses power only for personal gain or impact" in contrast to "uses power to serve others", or the more dubious "promotes own personal vision" in contrast to "aligns vision with followers' needs and aspirations", and so forth. The curious part is that one would expect a charismatic leader to be able to persuade others into believing that power was used to serve, and accordingly one would expect everyone would see eye to eye with the leader's vision, if the expression may be pardoned. As has happened under regimes with charismatic leaders.

It just goes to show that neither by using these characteristics nor anything else, can one really escape the ambiguity that is part of rule-violation and -creation.

The important thing about the dynamic trying-to-change response is that it represents a way of consciously trying to change existing ethical rules found wanting, or even first steps towards the creation of new rules more fitting to a society or an organization that has changed.

Maybe it is the way all our ethical rules were created, rules bound to some duty, rules for calculating the utility of utility-based rules, rules based on power. Their time-independent character may be a result of forgetfulness. We have forgotten the purpose of the rules or we may just have learned the rules, but never thought about the reason for them, or the conditions of their creation, and now they lie there semi-submerged in our consciousness, ready to influence, or even decide, the response we give when presented with an ethical dilemma.

---

17 HOWELL/AVOLIO (1992).

VIII. The Bestial Power Response

The president of ARMLIMO plc is asked what he is going to do, now that it has been made public that the local council is going to demand that ARMLIMO reduce the amount of pollutants emitted by half to protect the local environment. His answer: "The last time they came to me with that demand, I told them in a friendly manner that I would either close or move the plant, and by and by they found a solution acceptable to us, although I believe they had a bit of explaining to do in their political hinterlands".

Here power shows its face, power based on the fact that one is able to decide whether to close or move plant, when somebody demands that one should obey some rules. In this case the local council certainly did something they would not otherwise have done, they changed the rules under the influence of power.

ARMLIMO violates the rules then, and so what? What is the difference between this and the so-called dynamic trying-to-change response? Is it not the same kind of will-to-power that we see in action here? The answer is not all that clear; it depends. It depends on the reasons lying behind the use of power and the interests it serves. From a lust stemming from using it, through self-interest, the interest of the firm, to a conviction that one is doing the right thing, and being able to do it is just good fortune. Sometimes we seem to need people driven by "Unternehmungslust, Tollkühnheit, Rachsucht, Verschlagenheit, Raubgier, Herrsucht"[18]. At other times, it is precisely these driving forces that we try to curb by ethical rules.

In the cases where power is used because one has power or because it furthers one's self-interest, the response does not fall into the category of a dynamic trying-to-change response. In this case power reigns supreme. More difficult are the cases where conviction supports the use of power. This does not seem at all different from the response in the former section. Differentiating between having power and the will-to-power might help us clear the issue. Having power or being in power may influence the way one judges duty and utility, more or less according to Lord Acton's formula that power corrupts and absolute power corrupts absolutely. Duty and utility may then be bent and, as a consequence, duty and utility may support the views held by those in power.

18 NIETZSCHE (1886), p. 89.

This might not only be a matter of personal conviction. Having this kind of power enables one to influence the meaning of duty and utility for people dependent on the power one possesses. The relationship might be expressed like this: "We are strong because our cause is the only just cause (as seen in the Bible, the Koran, or whatever)" or "We are right, because we have the power (the gun, the bomb, or whatever)". This is the bestial face of power. This is the power that creates the values, supporting it in such a way that it makes the powerful even more powerful, because appeals to duty and utility support it instead of containing it. In figure 2:6 this relation between power, duties and utility considerations is illustrated.

Figure 2:6

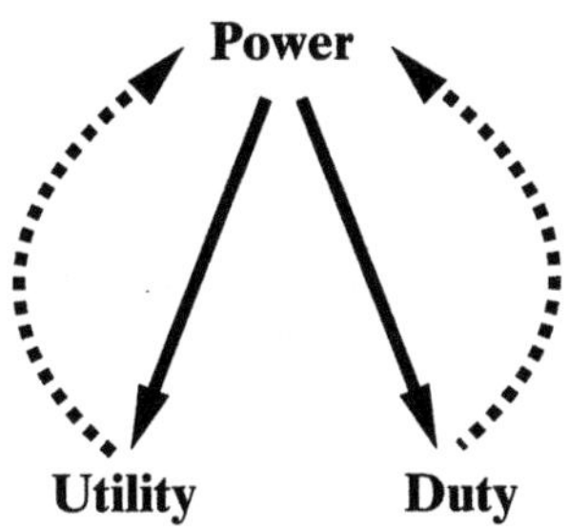

This relation may be found in authoritarian regimes, but more important to us, it may emerge in every type of organization. It may even emerge in a seemingly benevolent way, through the convincing actions of a charismatic leader, using his or her charisma, to enlarge his or her power and influence. This may represent the negative side of charismatic personalities. It may stand for some of the Destructive Achievers that Kelly talks about[19].

IX. Ethics – Protection or Prison

Now we have seen some of the possible responses and the reasoning, or lack thereof, behind them, but in what way do the different responses

19 KELLY (1987).

influence a given society, or just a company? Do they act as a form of protection against certain kinds of behaviour, do they act as the bars of a prison, or do they actively promote change by transgressing existing rules?

How is the rule following protection of the "good" secured? By control and sanctions, by imitation, by self-command, or by force? And how can rules seen as bars be transgressed? By evading control and sanctions, by imitating rule-violating behaviour, by lack of self-command, or willpower and force?

Once more, we have grouped the different response combinations and tried to characterize their effects in upholding rules or destroying and changing rules (Table 2:1).

Looking at the control and sanctions response, it should be clear that sufficient control and severe sanctions protect a certain order, certain values and power relations. It also seems clear that an amount of rules sufficient to safeguard against the self-interest will tend to result in a kind of transparent state with an enormous control apparatus, or in the case of a company, in a company dominated by control procedures and heavily burdened by the cost of control. In this case, the rules may in fact become all too real bars of a prison.

Table 2:1

Response combinations	Effect
The control and sanctions response	Upholds or destroys
The imitative adjustment response	Neutral
The pragmatic or cyclical-undetermined response	Neutral
The static trying-to-uphold respons	Upholds
The dynamic trying-to-change response	Changes
The bestial power response	Upholds or changes

If only the rules exist but the control and sanctions system has not been developed because nobody wants it, or because of the cost, one will experience rule violations in ever- spreading spirals. Self-interest will by and by be the almost sole determinant of behaviour, and rule-violations will be the order of the day. Until presumably everyone feels that this is not the best way, being hit by the consequences of everyone else acting according to their self-interests, and attempts to create or resurrect rules may be initiated.

The imitative adjustment response, on the other hand, is neutral in this respect. One may unknowingly contribute to the spreading of unethical behaviour, destroying the cement of society[20], or one may, again unknowingly, contribute to spreading of a set ethical values and ethical behaviour.

The same thing may happen in the case where one uses a pragmatic or cyclical-undetermined response. What happens is that one is aware of what is going on but discounts one's own influence on that. One actively adapts to and promotes the values dominating a society, or a company.

In the case of the static trying-to-uphold response, one is actively seeking to uphold the existing order of things, by appeals to the existing ethical rules. By appealing to something that may seem always relevant, always right, always good. This does not only go for the duty-bound response, but also for the utilitarian calculation, because the calculation is, by definition, based on existing valuations, as in a cost-benefit analysis.

In the dynamic trying-to-change response one actively seeks to change existing valuations and existing rules in order to create new rules. It is important to note that in contrast to the rule-violations connected to the first response, we now experience rule-violations based on conscious reasoning, or deeply-felt beliefs. Here the existing rules are seen as bars to be broken and cast aside.

The bestial power response, of course, can be related to the safeguarding of a certain order, but it can also be related to change, to change based on the lust for power and influence, or even based on something like a sense of a mission. In this case, though, the rules may soon degenerate into the bars of a prison.

If the premises behind this table are accepted, it should be evident that when we usually talk about ethics, we talk about rule-following

20 ELSTER (1989a).

behaviour, not really questioning the rules as such. Strictly speaking, what we are promoting is conscious rule-following responses to ethical problems, that is to say responses, that uphold some existing order of things.

What seems to be forgotten is that responses to ethical problems may in most cases be control and sanctions responses or simply imitative behaviour without really knowing why.

Although perhaps surprising, it should also be evident that in order to stay ethical, as it were, rules have to be broken. Broken, that is, through a conscious change of behaviour, using arguments relating to the reasons given in the section discussing the dynamic trying-to-change response.

Finally we may ask: which combinations are relevant for our ethical decisions and actions? Can the decisions and actions of some individuals and firms be understood by reference to a specific combination? That would mean we should be able to classify individuals and firms according the combination they seem to use. In what may seem a far-fetched analogy to some of the ideas found in strategic management literature, one might then talk of innovators, imitators, followers, and defenders, or even entrepreneurs and champions of ideas.

Another way of looking at it might be to see our decisions and actions as being guided by different combinations at different moments in time or in different situations. That would mean that we would be able to classify the ethical responses according to the combination that might explain them. This way of looking at the different combination seems more promising and it does not exclude the possibility of classifying individuals and firms at a later time if their responses seem to follow from a certain combination.

X. Conclusion

A delicate balance of duties, utilities and power considerations seems to govern our responses to ethical problems, if we think about it.

In our everyday experience we walk a tightrope between the experiences of the past, which are fixed in inflexible ethical rules, and the demands of the present, which demand dynamic changes in those very rules.

Even so, most of our responses may be ethically unaware, just calculating risk of discovery, and severity of sanctions or, even simpler, just imitating what others do.

References

AXELROD, R.: *The Evolution of Cooperation*, New York (Basic Books) 1984.

BENTHAM, J.: *An Introduction to the Principles of Morals and Legislation.* (1789), edited by J. H. BURNS and H. L. A. HART, *The Collected Works of Jeremy Bentham*, London (The Athlone Press) 1970.

BODEN, M.: *The Creative Mind: Myths and Mechanisms,* London (Weidenfeld and Nicolson) 1990.

BUCHANAN, A.: *Ethics, Efficiency, and the Market*, Totowa, New Jersey (Rowman and Allanheld) 1985.

CARR, A.: "Is Business Bluffing Ethical?", *Harvard Business Review,* 46 (January/February) 1968.

DONALDSON, T., A. R. GINI: *Case Studies in Business Ethics,* Englewood Cliffs, New Jersey (Prentice Hall) 1990.

ELSTER, J.: *The Cement of Society – A Study of Social Order,* Cambridge (Cambridge University Press) 1989 a.

ELSTER, J.: *The Market and the Forum – Three varieties of political theory. In Foundations of Social Choice Theory*, edited by J. ELSTER and A. HYLLAND, Cambridge (Cambridge University Press/Universitetsforlaget) 1989 b.

HOSMER, LARUE T.: *The Ethics of Management,* Boston, MA (Irvin) 1991.

HOWELL, J., B. AVOLIO: "The Ethics of Charismatic Leadership: Submission or Liberation", *The Executive,* 6 (1992), pp. 43–54.

KANT, I.: *Ethical Philosophy – The complete texts of the Grounding for the Metaphysics of Morals and Metaphysical Principles of Virtue* (1785), translated by JAMES W. ELLINGTON, Indianapolis, Indiana (Hackett) 1983.

KELLY, C.: "The Interrelationship of Ethics and Power in Today's Organizations", *Organizational Dynamics,* 16 (1987), no 1, pp. 5–17.

LUKES, S.: *Power – A Radical View*, London (Macmillan) 1974.

MACHIAVELLI, N.: *The Prince. In Machiavelli — The Prince, selections from The Discourses and other writings* (1513), edited by J. PLAMENATZ, London (Fontana/Collins).

NIETZSCHE, F.: *Jenseits von Gut und Böse.*(1886), Berlin (Goldmann) 1989.

Part Two

Reports from the Field

Chapter 3

Business Ethics and the Financial Community

LARS BERGKVIST

During the last few years the financial markets in many countries have exhibited several scandals ranging from insider trading to breach of trust committed by e.g. managing directors on the stockholders. In Sweden there are at the moment one very well media covered trial regarding breach of trust and several investigations on suspected insider trading. One expression of the changes in public opinion in Sweden is the new insider legislation, enacted about a year ago, which is far more comprehensive than the old legislation.

Are the spectacular events presented in the newspapers exceptions from generally good ethical conduct or are the ethical standards in the financial community indeed very low? In relation to this it is relevant to pose the question of how real examples of low ethics are judged and what ethical attitudes the prevailing standards in the financial community foster.

This study draws heavily on an earlier study carried out during 1988. That study is presented in Westlund[1] and Wärneryd and Westlund[2].

1 WESTLUND (1991).

2 WÄRNERYD/WESTLUND (1991).

Both studies were carried out with mail surveys. The core of the questionnaires were seven (six in the earlier study) vignettes based on actual events. The respondents were asked to judge the ethicality, frequency and legality of the events depicted in the vignettes.

I. The Purpose of the Study

There were three purposes with the present study[3]:

to investigate ethical attitudes and judgments of ethical conduct in the financial community

to compare a group of business school students, a sample of financial analysts and a sample of financial journalists

to test a causal structural model of ethical judgments proposed in Wärneryd and Westlund[4]

1. Empirical Studies of Business Ethics

Randall and Gibson[5] studied the methodology of 94 published articles on empirical business ethics between 1961 and 1989. The most common method is mail surveys using questionnaires where respondents are asked to judge hypothetical situations or report their own or others ethical behaviour. To some extent laboratory experiments or depth interviews have been employed.

Two factors are very important to the validity of empirical studies of business ethics. The respondents must be involved in the issue of business ethics[6] and they must feel assured of anonymity for themselves and their firm[7]. The latter speaks for the use of mail surveys and against the use of depth interviews.

3 The first two purposes are, apart from the samples, identical with the purposes presented in Wärneryd /Westlund (1991).

4 This part of the research is not presented in this paper as the analysis of the data collected merely has begun.

5 Randall/Gibson (1990).

6 Wärneryd/Westlund (1991).

7 Randall/Fernandes (1991).

Randall and Gibson[8] point out several weaknesses with the reviewed studies. Several lack a theoretical framework, few test any hypotheses and important concepts are rarely defined. Few articles discuss the validity and the reliability of the employed measures. Finally the response rates were typically low (on average 43%) and very simple methods were used in the data analyses.

The bulk of empirical research in business ethics has been carried out during the last six or seven years. So far researchers have not agreed entirely on methods and few, if any, well tested instruments exist.

One of the few major empirical studies that has been carried out in Sweden is the study done by Kristin Westlund[9]. See below for details.

2. The Ethics of Business Students

As in many other social sciences business ethics researchers frequently investigate the attitudes and perceptions of students. Kraft and Singhapakdi[10] investigated the differences in ethical perceptions between business students and service–sector managers. They found that students rated the importance of ethical conduct and some dimensions of social responsibility lower than managers. The results from Westlund's study[11] showed that students made more lenient judgments of unethicality than financial managers.

Some regard the indications of lower ethics among business school students as a bad sign for the future. Tomorrow's managers will behave much less ethical than the managers of today. This view of students' attitudes toward ethical issues considers the difference as a difference between generations. Worry about the bad behaviour of the next generation is probably as old as mankind and it appears to be a very narrow minded approach. It excludes the possibility that some kind of individual development occurs.

Some business ethics research based on Kohlberg's model of cognitive moral development (CMD) has been carried out[12]. This model focuses on the cognitive decision–making process and the ability for moral reasoning. According to the model important factors for the development of

8 RANDALL/GIBSON (1990).
9 WESTLUND (1991).
10 KRAFT/SINGHAPAKDI (1991).
11 WESTLUND (1991).
12 e.g. DAVIS/WELTON (1991), GOOLSBY/HUNT (1992), PENN/COLLIER (1985), TREVINO (1986).

skill in moral reasoning is age and formal education[13]. Other researchers, with a different approach, have also found age to be an important factor for ethical judgments[14]. Both Goolsby and Hunt[15] and Trevino[16] contend that work experience may be an important factor for moral development. As a professional you have to balance the interests and welfare of several groups, a process which favour principled thinking in ethical issues.

Wärneryd and Westlund[17] stress that business executives, contrary to students, belong to organizations and professional associations which have, formal or informal, standards of conduct. The same authors argue that it is possible that managers base their judgments on emotions derived from practical experience with business ethical issues, while students' judgments are of a more cognitive nature.

Thus there are several explanations for the more lenient ethical judgments of students. If ethical judgments and decisions are regarded as based on ability, professional standards and emotions derived from practical experience, research and education can focus on these, and other relevant factors, instead of complaining about the youth of today.

3. Gender Differences in Ethical Attitudes and Judgments

Much research has been carried out on the difference in ethics between men and women. A common assumption is that women have higher ethical standards than men. Tsalikis and Ortiz–Bounafina[18] found no gender differences, while Ruegger and King[19] found that gender is a significant factor in the determination of ethical conduct. Women were more ethical than men.

4. Westlund's Study

Westlund's research was carried out during 1988 and is reported in Westlund[20] and in [21]Wärneryd and Westlund. As mentioned earlier, the

13 GOOLSBY/HUNT (1992).
14 e.g. RUEGGER/KING (1992).
15 *op. cit.*
16 TREVINO (1986).
17 WÄRNERYD/WESTLUND (1991).
18 TSALIKIS/ORTIZ–BOUNAFINA (1990).
19 RUEGGER/KING (1992).
20 WESTLUND (1991).
21 WÄRNERYD/WESTLUND (1991).

study was carried out with a mail survey. The respondents were financial managers or in charge of the finances of the 80 largest firms listed on the Stockholm Stock Exchange. A sample of third year students at the Stockholm School of Economics was used as a comparison group. The response rate was 56.9% in the business executive sample and 49.6% in the student sample.

The first part of the questionnaire consisted of six vignettes, each depicting an actual event from the Swedish financial world. The respondents were asked to judge the degree of unethicality, the perceived frequency of the described events in Sweden, the perceived frequency in western industrial countries and the legality of each situation outlined in the vignette. The second part of the questionnaire consisted of a number of attitude statements and several background variables.

The results of the study showed that students made more lenient judgments than executives. Further a strong relationship between perceived illegality and ethical judgment was found. Perception of illegality led to a harsh judgment of unethicality.

A relationship between perceived frequency and ethical judgment was found as well. Perception of high frequency of behaviour led to more lenient judgments. The attitude statements in the second part of the questionnaire were used to form indices of ethical attitude. Separate factor analyses on the two samples revealed four meaningful indices for each sample. The factor scores were used in regression analysis with ethical judgment as dependent variable. The attitude scores contributed to explain the variance in ethical judgments, but the strength of the relationship differed between the judgments of the different vignettes. The background variables were somewhat too limited in scope to be of much use in the explanation of ethical judgments.

5. A Model of Ethical Judgments

Based on Westlund's research, Wärneryd and Westlund (1991) sketched a tentative model of ethical judgments (figure 3:1). According to the model, an individual's education and experience influence his/her attitude toward ethical issues. Attitude influences perception of legality and frequency, which in turn influences the ethical judgment. It is also possible with a direct influence on ethical judgment by attitude.

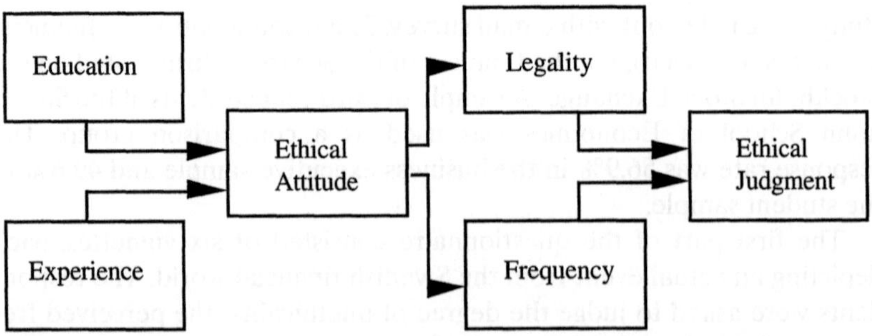

Figure 3:1. Factors Affecting Judgments of Unethical Behaviour. From Wärneryd and Westlund (1991).

There are several other factors which can be added to the model. For instance Terpstra et al.[22] found strong interaction effects between personality variables and situational variables. The personality variables tested were locus of control and interpersonal competitiveness, which interacted with perceptions of legality, action of others and profit potential. The measured variables and the interaction effects were found to be good predictors of insider trading in an experiment with business school students.

6. Ethical Judgments as Predictors of Ethical Behaviour

It is likely that many unethical and/or illegal actions are the result of a series of decisions and events. Cialdini[23] describes the process that led to the Watergate affair as a series of rejections and decisions where the final decision was a consequence of earlier steps in the process. Cialdini attributes the final decision taken to be a result of the influence of reciprocity and perceptual contrast.

Unethical and/or illegal behaviour could be described as the result of a process that consists of several innocent decisions which leads in the wrong direction. The decision makers get committed by earlier decisions

22 TERPSTRA et al. (1991).
23 CIALDINI (1988).

and finally wind up in a situation they could not have imagined to find themselves in. If ethical decision-making is a result of complicated processes, is there any value in investigating ethical attitudes and judgments?

In an attempt at a general theory of marketing ethics, Hunt and Vitell[24] include ethical judgments as an antecedent of intentions, which in turn is an antecedent of behaviour. Based on psychological theory and empirical research they contend that ethical judgments and intentions can be good predictors of behaviour, particularly when ethical issues are central.

Even if ethical judgment is limited as a predictor of individual behaviour, it is a very good means to measure ethical standards among groups of people and a study of the process that leads to judgment can provide several useful insights.

7. The Present Study

The present study draws on Westlund's study[25]. However, several changes has been made in the questionnaire and the samples were drawn from new target groups. To make a comparison with the earlier study possible five of the six vignettes were used unchanged and all but one of the attitude statements. Two new vignettes and several attitude statements were added. A new part of the questionnaire contained statements on personality variables and several new background variables were included.

8. The Questionnaire

The questionnaire contained seven vignettes, each depicting an actual business event. The first five vignettes were written by Mr. Sten Wikander, former head of one of the largest pension funds in Sweden and with much experience of the Swedish financial world. These vignettes were also included in Westlund's study. Two new vignettes were written by the author of this paper with very valuable advice from a reference group on ethical matters formed by the Center for Business and Policy Studies.

24 HUNT/VITELL (1986).

25 WESTLUND (1991).

The respondents were asked to judge four aspects of the events described in each vignette. Whether the event was an example of lacking ethics, whether the event is frequently occurring in Swedish industry, whether the event is frequently occurring in western industrial countries and whether the event is legal or illegal. For the first three items a ten–point scale was used and for the legal/illegal aspect a five–point scale was used.

Several aspects of attitudes toward business ethics were measured with 31 statements. Nine statements were made to measure personality variables. The responses were measured on a five–point agree–disagree scale. 19 questions regarding background variables were asked to the professionals sample and 19 background questions were asked to the student sample.

9. The Samples

Three samples were used for the study. The target groups were financial analysts, financial journalists and business students likely to work in the financial world.

A random sample of one third of the members (231 people) of the Swedish Society for Financial Analysts was drawn. The society is a professional association which demand that prospective members have at least one year professional experience of financial analysis.

The journalist sample was made up of a list of journalists who had requested to obtain financial information from a financial information firm in Stockholm. After deletion of those journalists who lived abroad or had changed jobs the list contained 65 names.

The student sample consisted of 121 third year students at Stockholm School of Economics specializing in Financial Economics, Accounting and Finance or Economic Analysis and Control during the academic year 1991–1992.

The overall response rate for professionals was 66% (N=196). Of these 40 stated their profession as financial journalist and 151 were financial analysts. Five respondents did not state any profession. The response rate for financial analysts was 65% and for financial journalists 62%. 89 students answered which gave a response rate of 73%.

II. Results

1. A Comparison of the Ethical Judgments of the Three Groups

The respondents were asked to judge whether the situation depicted in the vignettes was an example of deficient ethics (10 = to a very high degree an example of deficient ethics and 1 = not at all an example of deficient ethics). The mean scores for each vignette for the different groups are presented in table 1.

The students' judgments were more lenient on all vignettes except no. 2 ("oral agreement"). The differences were highly significant in four cases. These results were consistent with the results of the earlier study.

A comparison between the students' judgments of the five vignettes that were included in both studies reveal no significant differences except for case 2 which was judged somewhat harsher in the present study (8.45 compared with 7.78).

A comparison between the judgments of the analysts and the journalists indicated no systematic difference.

Table 3:1. Mean Scores on Ethical Judgment Scales

Case	Students	Analysts	Journalists	F
1."insider trading"	7.29	8.35	9.23	10.96
2."oral agreement"	8.45	8.21	8.05	0.59****
3."private interests"	7.02	9.29	8.49	33.44****
4 "insider tips"	7.84	9.74	9.65	45.20****
5."minority interests"	5.24	5.64	5.69	0.59
6."risky debt"	7.42	7.47	7.45	0.01
7."breach of trust"	7.74	9.54	9.15	26.83****

****P<0.001 ***P>0.01 **P>0.05 *P>0.10

The high average judgments of unethicality in the analyst and journalist samples indicate that the prevailing ethical standards are very strict. The average judgments in the student sample were lower for all cases except case 2. The difference could be an expression of more lenient norms among students, but it is more probable that students as a group have no business ethical standards, and that their judgments are based solely on self-governed cognitive elaboration.

A comparison between the judgments of the analysts and journalists and the judments of the financial managers in Westlund's study showed that case three was somewhat harsher judged in the present study (9.29 and 8.49 compared with 8.10), and the same applies to case 4 (9.74 and 9.65 compared with 8.23).

2. Perception of Frequency in the Three Groups

The respondents were asked to judge the frequency in Sweden of the events depicted in the vignettes (where 10 = frequent and 1 = does not occur at all). The mean scores for each group on each case is reported in table 3:2.

There was an overall tendency for the students to judge the described behaviours as more frequently occurring. The judgements of the analysts and journalists were similar, except in case 4.

Table 3:2. Mean Scores on Frequency in Sweden Scales

Case	Students	Analysts	Journalists	F
1."insider trading"	6.65	6.43	6.38	0.33
2."oral agreement"	5.01	5.43	5.33	1.16
3."private interests"	5.60	4.89	4.94	3.48**
4 "insider tips"	6.07	4.61	5.62	11.42****
5."minority interests"	6.13	5.51	5.69	2.55*
6."risky debt"	7.19	6.80	7.10	0.93
7."breach of trust"	5.47	4.99	5.41	1.48

****P<0.001 ***P>0.01 **P>0.05 *P>0.10

The respondents were asked to judge the frequency of the events in western industrialized countries on a similar scale. There was a weak tendency in the student sample to judge the described behaviours as more frequently occurring abroad. The differences were small, however. There is no clear tendency in two professional groups. A comparison with

Westlund's results showed no significant differences between the two student samples, but there was a tendency among analysts and journalist to judge the events as more frequently occurring than the financial managers.

It is impossible to tell whether the differences in both ethical judgment and perceived frequency between the professional groups in the two studies depended on different ethical standards in the groups or if it was a result of changes that have occurred during the time that has passed between the two studies, e.g. there have been many newspaper reports of unethical behaviour in the financial world during the last few years which may have contributed to a perception of increased frequency.

It is noteworthy that the students both perceived the described events as more frequently occurring and at the same time judged them as less unethical. This indicates a gap between students' view of the financial world and the view held by those actually working in the financial world.

3. Perception of Illegality

The final question asked about the vignettes was whether the described behaviour was legal or illegal. The responses were measured on a scale where 5 = the behaviour is illegal and 1 = the behaviour is legal. The mean scores for each group are reported in table 3:3.

Table 3:3. Mean Scores on Illegal – Legal Scales

Case	Students	Analysts	Journalists	F
1."insider trading"	3.29	3.35	3.23	0.13
2."oral agreement"	3.47	2.87	2.23	9.80****
3."private interests"	2.29	2.89	2.08	9.05****
4 "insider tips"	3.82	4.48	4.10	9.31****
5."minority interests"	1.94	1.63	1.84	2.54*
6."risky debt"	2.57	2.21	2.00	2.89*
7."breach of trust"	3.40	4.25	3.77	12.92****

****P<0.001 ***P>0.01 **P>0.05 *P>0.10

As a check whether the students' more lenient judgment were a result of young age and not lack of work–experience a comparison with the judgments of young (age < 30 years) analysts and journalist was made. There were 23 young professionals in the sample which were compared with 89 students. The results are presented in table 3:4.

Table 3:4. Differences in Ethical Judgments Between Students and Young Professionals

Case	Students	Young P.	T
1."insider trading"	7.29	8.59	– 2.69***
2."oral agreement"	8.45	7.78	1.27
3."private interests"	7.02	9.05	– 4.31****
4 "insider tips"	7.84	9.87	– 7.52****
5."minority interests"	5.24	6.09	– 1.18
6."risky debt"	7.42	7.61	– 0.29
7."breach of trust"	7.74	9.78	– 6.97****

****P<0.001 ***P>0.01 **P>0.05 *P>0.10

Table 3:5. Differences in Ethical Judgments Between Men and Women

Case	Men	Women	T
1."insider trading"	8.37	9.08	2.24**
2."oral agreement"	8.03	8.86	2.77***
3."private interests"	9.14	8.89	– 0.71
4 "insider tips"	9.71	9.72	0.11
5."minority interests"	5.36	6.89	2.71***
6."risky debt"	7.44	7.47	0.05
7."breach of trust"	9.48	9.36	– 0.42

****P<0.001 ***P>0.01 **P>0.05 *P>0.10

4. The Ethical Judgments of Parents

In one of the background questions the respondents were asked if they were parents or not. In the professionals samples 116 people were parents and 75 were not (below referred to as non-parents). A comparison of the ethical judgments of the two groups is presented in table 6.

Parents made significantly harsher judgments on cases 2 and 6. The judgments of the other cases were not significantly different between the groups, but the possibility that bringing up children fosters a somewhat more ethical attitude cannot be ruled out.

Table 3:6. Differences in Ethical Judgments Between Parents and Non-parents.

Case	Parents	Non-parents	T
1."insider trading"	8.46	8.55	-0.29
2."oral agreement"	8.42	7.81	1.86*
3."private interests"	9.09	9.10	-0.04
4 "insider tips"	9.72	9.68	0.29
5."minority interests"	5.90	5.22	1.50
6."risky debt"	7.83	6.83	2.56**
7."breach of trust"	9.37	9.57	-0.98

****P<0.001 ***P>0.01 **P>0.05 *P>0.10

5. Discussion

The results from this study supports the findings of several earlier studies that students' attitudes to ethical issues are different from professionals'. As mentioned earlier in this paper there are several possible reasons for this. An indication of the importance of work–experience is given by the results of the comparison between students and young professionals. Wärneryd and Westlund[26] point out that real life can

26 WÄRNERYD/WESTLUND (forthcoming).

turn out to be a shocking experience to theoretically trained graduates because of the wide gap between theory and practice.

Possible implications for the teaching of business ethics at business schools would be to try to narrow the gap between theory and practice, e.g. by inviting professionals to teach.

Some indications that women and parents have a more strict view of ethical dilemmas were found. The findings were too weak to draw any conclusions, but it could be fruitful to look into the attitudes and judgments of these groups more thoroughly.

References

CIALDINI, R. B.: *Influence. Science and Practice*, Glenview, Illinois (Scott, Foresman and Company) [2]1988.

DAVIS, J. R., R. E. WELTON: "Professional Ethics: Business Students' Perceptions", *Journal of Business Ethics,* 10 (1991), pp. 451–463.

GOOLSBY, J., R. HUNT, D. SHELBY: "Cognitive Moral Development and Marketing", *Journal of Marketing* (1992), pp. 55–68.

HUNT, R., D. SHELBY, S. VITELL: "A General Theory of Marketing Ethics", *Journal of Macromarketing,* 1 (1986), pp. 5–16.

KRAFT, L., A. SINGHAPAKDI: "The Role of Ethics and Social Responsibility in Achieving Organizational Effectiveness: Students Versus Managers", *Journal of Business Ethics* (1991), pp. 679–686.

PENN, JR., W. Y., COLLIER, B. D.: "Current Research in Moral Development as a Decision Support System", *Journal of Business Ethics* (1985), pp. 131–136.

RANDALL, D. M., FERNANDES, M. F.: "The Social Desirability Response Bias in Ethics Research", *Journal of Business Ethics* (1991), pp. 805–817.

RANDALL, D. M., GIBSON, A. M.: "Methodology in Business Ethics Research: A Review and Critical Assessment", *Journal of Business Ethics* (1990), pp. 457–471.

RUEGGER, D., KING, E. W.: "A Study of the Effect of Age and Gender upon Student Business Ethics", *Journal of Business Ethics* (1992), pp. 179–186.

TERPSTRA, D. E., REYES, M.G.C., BOKOR, D. W.: "Predictors of Ethical Decisions Regarding Insider Trading", *Journal of Business Ethics* (1991), pp. 699–710.

TREVINO, KLEBE, L.: "Ethical Decision Making in Organizations: A Person–Situation Interactionist Model", *Academy of Management Review* (1986), pp. 601–617.

TSALIKIS, J., M. ORTIZ-BUONAFINA: "Ethical Beliefs' Differences of Males and Females", *Journal of Business Ethics* (1990), pp. 509–517.

WESTLUND, K.: *Affärsetik. En studie av etiska bedömningar* (Business Ethics. A Study of Ethical Judgments). Research Report, Stockholm (The Economic Research Institute) 1991.

WÄRNERYD, K-E, WESTLUND, K.: *Ethical Issues in the World of Finance: An Empirical Study*, unpublished manuscript (1991).

Chapter 4

Moral Support Structures in Swedish Industry

TOMAS BRYTTING

I. Introduction

Jacob Wallenberg once commented on a business proposal with these words; "It may be legally correct but it's not musical". What he apparently wanted to say was that the proposal did not follow his understanding of proper business. However, a more elaborate formulation of proper business, other than that it is "musical", seemed to be lacking. If guided only by this vague description, decision-makers within his organization must have felt quite frustrated when faced with the challenge to develop the same good ear as the old banker.

Mr Wallenberg belonged to a generation of business leaders who might have shared a common idea of proper, or for that matter unproper business behaviour. Today, nobody can claim to have an absolute (moral) pitch. A community of values within business and worklife is being questioned – if it ever existed. Instead competing values and norms appear in business as well as in worklife.

At the same time, efficient management rests today more than ever on some kind of common corporate values. A modern decentralized work-organization is built on the assumption that human beings contribute with energy, creativity and motivation if the goals and basic principles of the organization is understood and shared by all members. In such an organization the amount of direct supervision, monitoring and regulation can be minimized; the image of a high-performing low-cost organization. This might be the reason why an increasing number of companies, also in Sweden, introduce more or less formal means to control and support the "musical ear" of their employees. Another reason might be the increased risk of legal punishments being laid on business organizations if their employees violate the law. Edward Petry Jr.[1] reports that U.S. companies' legal responsibility "to maintain internal mechanisms for preventing, detecting and reporting criminal conduct" has been notified by the U.S. Sentencing Commission. Judges may, however, reduce legal fines if the company have, e.g. "established standards and procedures for employees and other agents that are reasonably capable of reducing the prospect of criminal conduct, specific individual(s) with responsibility to oversee compliance, methods for communicating standards and procedures such as training programs and publications..." With due respect to all the differences in legal structures and traditions, Swedish managers may experience similar driving forces.

In the above quotation we recognize four of the most common business ethics instruments; ethics codes, ethics officers, ethics committees and ethics courses. We believe that managers take these kinds of action, for one reason or the other, to support, influence or manipulate the value system that determine so much of what goes on in their companies. At the same time very little is known about how frequent these measures are. In this paper we therefore take a closer look at explicit managerial ethics tools, or "moral support structures". We want to capture how Swedish industry deals with business ethics.

1. Research Objectives

Business ethics is concerned with how ethical values interfere with, or unite with commercial values. Thus, business ethics investigates, for instance, the interplay between personal dignity (an ethical value) and profits (a commercial value) from both theoretical and empirical perspectives.

1 Petry (1992).

The aim of this study is to investigate to what extent, and how companies engage in formal activities devoted to business ethics. We have limited the investigation to include only private companies in Sweden with more than one employee. Four types of moral support structures have been studied: The Code of Ethics, The Ethics Officer, The Ethics Committee and The Ethics Course.

How frequent are these moral support structures?
Which companies engage in them?
What do they contain?
What are the results?

The first two questions have been studied through a nation-wide telephone-survey and will be discussed in this paper. The latter two questions are studied in a follow-up postal survey which is still in progress. This second survey is directed to those companies that has some kind of moral support structure. We investigate more closely their content and the experiences companies have from working with them.

2. Why Structures?

We will make a special effort to explore the idea that moral support structures are one tool in the managers' tool-box. For instance, in the traditional factory employee conduct can be closely monitored and controlled by plans, technical means and by detailed job-descriptions. In the service industries these administrative tools loose some of their adequacy. If "production" takes place in the direct meeting with the customer, sometimes even at the customer's premises, bureaucratic control methods; e.g. detailed specifications, direct supervision or technical control, will be inefficient. What we envision is – in Ouchi's[2] terms – a shift from a bureaucratic to a "clan" type of workorganization as the character of activities changes from material production to service. Compliance to rules is insufficient, instead internalization of values and beliefs becomes necessary prerequisites for success. This internalization of values can be supported by careful design of organizational structures. Thus, one might hypothesize that moral support structures of the kind we defined above,

2 Ouchi (1979).

are relatively more frequent in the service industry generally, and especially in service sub-industries where employees have direct customer-relations and do their work outside of direct monitoring.

It is almost a truism to say that moral values cannot be controlled by orders, and if modern management is dependent on a community of values, the importance and efficiency of structural measures by top-management in this area should be questioned. In opposition with this view, we will argue that moral values to a large extent are socially constructed. And in so far as socialization takes place at the workplace – i.e. in organizations – also moral values will be influenced by structural factors. The way in which structures influence the moral values of organizational members and their behaviour are quite complex. Sjöstrand[3] suggests five different functions of organization structures: Focus – helps the members to choose correct actions: Control – assessment and rewarding of individual performances; Identification – supports commitment of individuals to the organization; Legitimation – stresses that the organization is part of the surrounding value community and Reproduction – the organization as a manifestation of power relation. Moral support structures, we believe, are being introduced for all these reasons and deserve a closer description and scrutinization, also by researchers in business ethics.

3. Some Previous Studies

Descriptive surveys of how business ethics have been institutionalized are rare. Most studies we have found have been focused on codes of ethics. This is quite natural since these codes were among the first manifest and visible signs of a growing interest in ethics in business organizations.

Langlois and Schlegelmilch[4] investigated the 200 largest companies in France, Germany and the United Kingdom. They found that 41% of their sample said that they had a code of ethics. The figure in France was 30%, in the U.K. 41% and in Germany the figure was 51%. These figures are highly uncertain, though, and probably inflated since the responsrate was only 32%. A study by the Center for Business Ethics[5] in USA reports that 75% of the major U.S. corporations have codes of ethics.

3 Sjöstrand (1987).
4 Langlois/Schlegelmilch (1989).
5 Center for Business Ethics (1986).

Leonard Brooks[6] cites two Canadian studies where more than 50% of the largest companies were found to have codes of ethics.

Very few studies have been conducted on ethics committees. Feder mentions in an article in The New York Times[7] that more than 15% of U.S. Corporations employing more than 50.000 people have ethics offices, almost all created within the last five years.

Diana Robertson[8] reports that 53% of her US sample have written codes of ethics, 29% says they have "policy statements" and 43% that they have "guidelines." Of the largest companies in her sample (with more than 50.000 empl.) 16.2% have a "board of directors ethics committee." An ethics "Ombudsman" was found in 5% of the whole sample and 6% have a "Corporate Ethics Office." Ethics training was offered by 24% of the companies in her sample and 10% say that they train all their employees in ethics.

A major weakness with all of these studies, besides their consistently low response rates, is that they – from a European perspective – only study large companies, even if some of these companies are called "small." Robertson[9], for instance, labels companies with less than 1000 employees as "very small." As a contrast, consider the OECD size definitions which are radically different; companies are "very small" if they employ less than 20 people! The results from Robertson's and most other studies in this area can therefore not be generalized outside the large company sector of the economy. It is in fact questionable whether we know anything at all about how regular firms institutionalize business ethics. Developed countries generally have roughly half of their employment in firms with less than 100 employees[10], so the unexplored area is vast!

The only study of the Swedish situation was recently concluded by Ulrica Nylèn[11]. Her research is focused on managerial attitudes to ethical issues, but does also contain a question about codes of ethics. She reports that 15% of Swedish companies have written codes of ethics; the figure ranges from 0% for the smallest firms (<10 empl.), 20% for the medium

6 Brooks (1989).
7 Feder (1991).
8 Robertson (1989).
9 Robertson (1991).
10 Sengenberger/Loveman (1987).
11 Nylèn (1992).

sized firms (10-49 empl.) and 25% for firms with more than 50 employees. She also notes that the figure is considerably higher within the food retail-industry (25%) compared to the other industry sectors she studied (12% in both machine manifacturing and technical consulting).

4. The Study

The population in focus of this study was Swedish private companies with more than one employee. Some industries were excluded such as private education, research and medical service. One reason for this exclusion was that these services function in highly regulated "markets" where the dominance of commercial aspects might vary. Instead of business ethics, therefore, these services are more concerned with other fairly well defined areas of ethics, e.g. medical ethics. We also excluded the smallest firms within farming, forestry, hunting and fishing, for similar reasons; commercial aspects are but one part of their concerns. Finally, we excluded the smallest firms in the financial and real-estate industries. The reason was the suspicion that these "firms" mostly are private property registered as a firm for tax-reasons, but with no, or only restricted public operations.

The sampling frame was taken from Statistics Sweden's register of all Swedish companies, with the restrictions mentioned above. The frame was divided into three size strata (2–49, 50–199 and 200 or more employees) and eight industries using SNI-codes (a Swedish standard with similarities to the U.N. ISIC-system). These eight industries were:

1. Farming etc. (Farming, Forestry, Gardening, Hunting and Fishing)
2. Manufacturing (also including Mining and Power)
3. Building Industry
4. Wholesale and Retail
5. Communications (also including travel agencies)
6. Capital Managing (Banking, Insurance and Real-Estate)
7. Business Services (also including Machine Rental)
8. Other Service (Cleaning, Recreation, Maintenance)

These eight industries together with the three size strata formed a total of 24 strata. A weighted stratified sample was drawn from this sampling frame with the weights reflecting the size of the strata within the total population. The total sample drawn was 2,909 firms, 196 of which were excluded as duplicates, non-existent etc. Of the remaining 2,713 firms that were contacted, 2,313 answered our questions, forming a responsrate of 85%.

The study was conducted as a telephone-survey directed to the CEO or any other member of the top-management team. It contained five parts. First we asked about the ownership of the company. The alternatives were: Listed on the stock market, Subsidiary, Founder owned, Management owned, Employee owned, Externally private owned. The next four sets of questions concerned:

a) Codes of Ethics

"Do you have any written statement of your business ethics – for instance, a Code of Ethics or Business Principles? Which of the following types of ethics programmes or rules have you got in your company; written and distributed to the employees?

- The company's business concept
- A personnel policy
- Industry specific rules and regulations
- "Codes of Conduct"
- Business principles
- Other form of written rules"

"Would it not be correct to call these rules a form of written business ethic?"

b) Ethics Officer

"Do you have a person employed at your company with business ethics issues as part of his/her formal responsibility?"

c) Ethics Committees

"Do you have a special group or committee working with business ethics? How many times did this group meet last year?"

d) Training in Ethics

"Do you regularly send employees to business ethics courses? How many hours does that course include?"

Those companies that had a code of ethics were asked to send one copy to us. We also asked those companies that had engaged in any of these business ethics activities to give us the name of the person best suited to answer further questions.

II. Results

No less than 77.5% of the companies claim that they have some sort of formalized activity focused on business ethics issues. This figure is surprisingly high compared with other studies.

Tab 4:1. Percentage of firms within a certain strata that has a Code of Ethics, an Ethics Officer, an Ethics Committee and/or Training in Ethics.

	Firm size (nr. of empl):		
Industry sector:	2–49	50–199	200–
Farming etc.	–	75*	100*
Manufacturing	60	78	91
Building Industry	65	74	82
Wholesale and Retail	63	86	96
Communications	70	82	84
Capital Managing	–	94	97
Business Services	65	92	96*
Other Services	63	85	95*

(*=n<30)

Apart from the very high figures *per se*, we can also verify the hypothesis that moral support structures are more frequent in large firms than in small. This apply to all industries. The service sectors also shows slightly higher figures indicating an inclination towards structural measures of this kind.

The Code of Ethics

The first question we asked concerning codes of ethics was: "Do you have a written statement of your business ethics – for instance, a Code of Ethics or Business Principles?" 19% of the Swedish firms answer this question affirmatively. However, there are large differences between industry sectors and between small and large firms. Written codes of ethics are most common in the Capital Managing (62%) and Farming sectors (57%). The Building Industry and Communications sector form the other extreme (13%).

Tab 4:2. Percentage of firms within a certain strata that has a Code of Ethics.

	Firm size (nr. of empl.):		
Industry sector:	2–49	50–199	200–
Farming etc.	-	44*	100*
Manufacturing	16	25	46
Building Industry	13	34	52
Wholesale and Retail	19	45	64
Communications	13	30	50
Capital Managing	-	58	74
Business Services	30	58	58*
Other Services	17	45	45*
All industries	18	36	52

(*=n<30)

Of the smallest firms, with 2–49 employees, a total of 18 % say they have a code of ethics, a figure which is surprisingly high considering that earlier studies indicated that 15% among Swedish firms in general have a code of ethics. This figure increases rapidly with increased firm size (in all sectors); from 36% among middle sized firms, to 52% among the large companies. This places the large companies in Sweden at roughly the same level as those in Germany and the U.K.[12]

Ownership also influences the statistics. Companies listed on the stock market and subsidiaries tend to have codes to a large degree (52%

12 LANGLOIS/SCHLEGELMILCH (1989).

and 38%) while family-, management- or employee-owned firms are less likely to have a code of ethics (17%, 17% and 21%). This difference may, of course, disappear if the effect of firm size is eliminated.

Well aware of the fact that "ethics", "business ethics" and "codes of ethics" are unfamiliar concepts to most business people, we asked an additional question concerning other forms of written guidelines. When we presented alternative forms of documents to the companies, and asked if these contained ethical guidelines, many more of our respondents said they had written ethical guidelines. In the total sample, 41% of the companies now answered affirmatively on this issue. The Capital Managing and the Building Industry still form two extremes with 85% and 30% of the companies saying that they have written ethical guidelines.

The Ethics Officer

Maybe the most surprising finding from this study was the answer to the question about the Ethics Officer. We had expected this type of moral support structure to be very rare. Instead, no less than 45% of the companies claim that they have such a post in their organization.

Tab 4:3. Percentage of firms within a certain strata that have an Ethics Officer.

	Firm size (nr. of empl.):		
	2–49	50–199	200–
Industry sector:			
Farming etc.	-	37*	33*
Manufacturing	45	53	49
Building Industry	51	48	58
Wholesale and Retail	42	53	59
Communications	48	51	41
Capital Managing	-	60	65
Business Services	39	48	65*
Other Services	48	55	64*
All industries	44	52	53

(*=n<30)

This result may reflect a more generous interpretation among our respondents of "ethics officer" than the one we might have had in mind. What we asked was: "Do you have a person employed at your company with business ethics issues as part of his/her formal responsibility"? Probably some of the respondents had the general manager or the CEO in mind when they answered affirmatively on this question.

A closer investigation of this issue will be included in the second phase of this study. For the time being, we only want to point out that even if the high figures are inflated due to a vaguely specified question two things are worth noting. First, the service sectors show relatively higher figures. Secondly, firm size do not seem to influence the statistics so much. To explain this, we would suspect that respondents from small firms are more inclined to call the entrepreneur an Ethics Officer than respondants from larger companies, where "ethics" may be more readily connected to a professional, if not organizational specialty.

The Ethics Committee

"Do you have a special group or committee working with business ethics?" Previous research, however limited (see above), suggests that 15–16% of the large companies will answer affirmatively to this question. In our study, where also the smaller companies are included, 8% of the total sample say that they have such a group. There are however large differences between strata.

Tab 4:4. Percentage of firms within a certain strata that has an Ethics Committee.

	Firm size (nr. of empl.) :		
	2-49	50-199	200-
Industry sector:			
Farming etc.	-	19*	67*
Manufacturing	7	18	17
Building Industry	8	17	24
Wholesale and Retail	8	15	18
Communications	8	17	22
Capital Managing	-	18	35
Business Services	11	28	23*
Other Services	5	17	18*
All industries	8	18	19

(*=n<30)

We see clearly that the size factor is important, which was expected. For the larger companies in the sample, the figures are much higher than expected. The Capital Managing sector once again stands out as a sector were companies relatively frequently institutionalize ethics, but the larger companies within the Building Industry and Business Service also show high figures (24% and 23%).

The Farming etc. sector has an extremely high, but still significant figure for large companies since the total population in this strata is limited to three companies. (Our sample do not include the large producer and consumer cooperatives within this sector).

"To get a better understanding of the character of these committees we also asked: How many times did this group meet last year?" The generally high figures were surprising:

Tab 4:5. How many times did the Ethics Committee meet last year?

	Never	Once	Twice	3–4 times	5–6times	6 times or more
Farming*	–	–	26	16	26	33
Manufacturing	5	0	12	16	18	41
Building	0	–	1	17	17	49
Wholesale & Retail	0	6	0	12	17	42
Communications*	–	–	–	0	1	35
Capital Managing	–	–	3	10	10	50
Business Service	–	9	19	20	20	21
Other Service*	–	–	0	19	20	42
All industries	1	4	6	14	17	39

(*=n<30)

A surprisingly 39% of all Ethics Committees meet more often than every second month. The Business Service industry (but also Communications and Farming) is an exception with relatively low frequency of meetings.

Training in Ethics

The final question concerned to what extent Swedish companies regularly send their employees to ethics courses. The only available comparative figure was taken from Robertson (1989). She found that 24% of the large U.S. companies offers ethics training, 10% of them to all their employees. Given the difference in formulating our questions, the Swedish data shows similar, or somewhat lower results:

Tab 4:6 Percentage of firms within a certain strata that regurlarly send employees to Ethics Courses

Industry sector:	Firm size (nr. of empl.): 2–49	50–199	200–
Farming etc.	–	13*	–
Manufacturing	3	6	7
Building Industry	4	7	21
Wholesale and Retail	7	5	14
Communications	5	11	16
Capital Managing	5	23	
Business Services	3	13	23*
Other Services	11	8	5*
All industries	5	7	11

(*=n<30)

It appears that firm size is one explanatory factor, but less so than in the previous tables. In Other Services, for instance, firm size seems to have a negative correlation with ethics training.

As a follow-up question, we asked about the extent of these ethics courses or training sessions.

Tab 4:7. The extent of Ethics Courses offered to employees

	Firm size (nr. of empl.): 2–49	50–199	200–
less than 1/2 day	18	24	28
1/2 – one day	16	36	20
one day or more	56	36	42

The majority of the companies that offer ethics training to their employees do so by offering more than a few hours. Many companies, especially small firms tend to prefer training that goes on for at least a full day.

III. Discussion

1. Some Summarizing Reflections

This paper is the first attempt to present some of the findings of this study, and a more elaborate analysis and discussion of the results must have to wait. However, some questions can be raised already at this stage. We will start with a table that summarizes some of our findings:

Tab 4:8. Percentage of Swedish companies that have different sorts of Moral Support Structures

	Guidelines	Codes of Ethics	Officer	Committee	Training
Farming*	71	57	37	30	10
Manufacturing	38	18	46	8	4
Building	30	13	51	8	4
Wholesale & Retail	43	20	42	8	7
Communications*	41	13	48	8	5
Capital Managing	85	62	61	22	9
Business Service	54	31	40	12	4
Other Service*	38	18	48	6	11
All industries	41	19	45	8	6

(*=n>30)

The first striking observation is that the different moral support structures we have investigated, are much more common than we envisioned when we started this project. It is almost hard to believe that 77,5% of the Swedish companies have at least one of the four types of moral support structures. The frequency with which Ethics Committees have meetings and the extent of Ethics Training is also surprising to us. Second, the differences between industry sectors are striking. The sector we have labelled Capital Managing which contained Bank, Insurance and Real Estate, show high figures in all columns in this table. So does Farming. How can we understand these high figures and how do we explain them? Why do different industries "choose" different solutions?

For instance, does the presence of independent supervisory bodies within a certain industry sector – like the ones we find in Farming or Capital Managing – facilitate implementation of moral support structures within individual firms? The Building industry, on the other hand, guided as it is, at the work place, by elaborated technical standards and the professional's rules, may have less of a scope for company specific ethics activities. An interesting question is therefore: How does the presence, or absence, of non-ethics rules and regulations influence the probability that moral support structures will be introduced?

We mentioned in the beginning that organizational structures are introduced for many different reasons; legitimation and reproduction of power being two of them. The generally high figures coming out of this study, may simply be a result of the companies', or the managers' efforts to put forth a good image with little or no connection to practice. Still, the differences between industry sectors are there and begs for an explanation. Can it be that the need to make one's activities legitimate, differ so much between sectors that it explains our findings? This might be a plausible hypothesis, but at the same time, the low figures in the Building industry does not correspond to its very bad image in Sweden at present, after several accusations of bad workmanship, carelessness, bribes etc.

A third observation is the extent to which these support structures differ in "popularity". Written Codes of Ethics, which we thought was the most common moral support structure (because it is relatively cheap and simple to create) was found in 19% of all companies, while Ethics Officers obviously has been established in no less than 45% of the companies. Once again, though, this figure might be the result of a vaguely stated question and may change during the second stage of this research project. We would also have guessed ethical training to be more common than setting up an ethics committee. This was not the case. The neo-classic economists would say that this proves that ethics officers and codes of ethics do their job more cost-effectively than ethics training and ethics committees. But the question remains: What does it mean that they "do their job"? The "ranking" of support structures might instead be explained by visibility; the most visible structures are the most popular, suggesting that moral support structures are being introduced for PR, or legitimation reasons.

Fourth, the more general hypopthesis that large firms are more active in this field than small firms, were confirmed, but the differences were smaller than expected. Between 60 and 70% of the small firms in all industry sectors – and we talk about small firms with less than 50 employees – have some kind of moral support structure. We often hear that in the small firm, values are relatively homogenous, the internal communication is smooth and informal, public scrutinization is rare, resources are severally limited etc. and that this explains the many differences we find between small and large companies. If the differences are smaller than we thought, as in this study, for instance, maybe these small firm characteristics do not influence structure to the extent we commonly assume?

Finally, by asking a follow-up question on written guidelines, we managed to raise the figure from 19% to 41%. This might be an indication that managers, if given the opportunity, would like to say that they have ethics activities. Of course, this puts not only this study, but also some of the earlier research in perspective. How many percent of Swedish companies have a written ethical guideline? We do not at present have information that would allow us to discuss this question in detail. What we do know is that the definition of "codes of ethics" strongly influence the result one gets, and that reasons of legitimation probably play an important role when answering our questions.

2. The Second Stage

Further research, which is already taking place, will examine some of these issues more closely. Most of the companies in this study that had moral support structures, agreed to receive a more comprehensive survey. The idea with that survey is to get a better understanding of the content of these structural measures: How old are they? For what reasons were they created? What resources do they have at their disposal? How do they function? etc. We will also get the opportunity to ask about any visible efffects – if any. Some questions will be directed to clarify the content of the concepts "Codes of Ethics" and "Ethics Officer".

References

BROOKS, L.: "Corporate Codes of Ethics", *Journal of Business Ethics*, 8 (1989), no 2&3, pp 117–129.

CENTER FOR BUSINESS ETHICS: "Are corporations institutionalizing ethics?", *Journal of Business Ethics*, 5 (1986), no. 2, pp 85–91.

FEDER, B.: "Helping Corporate America Hew to the Straight and Narrow", *The New York Times*, November 3, 1991.

LANGLOIS, C., SCHLEGELMILCH, B.: "Do Corporate Codes of Ethics Reflect National Character", *The Journal of International Business Studies* (1990), pp 519–539.

NYLÈN, U.: "Företaget, Människan och Moralen – En undersökning av företagsledares attityder till etiska frågor inom affärslivet." Umeå Business School, 1992. See also "Ethical Views of Swedish Business Leaders", paper presented at the EBEN Conference on Business Ethics in a New Europe, London, 25–27 September, 1991.

OUCHI, W.: "A Conceptual Framework for the Design of Organizational Control Mechanisms", *Management Science*, 9 (1979), pp 833–848.

PETRY, E.: "The Federal Sentencing Guidelines For Organization", *Center for Business Ethics News*, 1 (1992), no 1, pp 4–5.

ROBERTSON, D.: "Corporate Ethics Programs: The Impact of Firm Size", in: HARVEY, B.,. VAN LUIJK, H, CORBETTA, G.: *Market Morality and Company Size*, Kluwer 1991.

SENGENBERGER, W., LOVEMAN, G.: "Smaller Units of Employment – A Synthesis Report on Industrial Reorganisation in Industrialised Countries." Discussion Papers. International Institute for Labour Studies, 1987 (rev. 1988)

SJÖSTRAND, S.-E.: "Organisationsteori", Studentlitteratur (1987), pp 155–173.

Chapter 5

Forming an Ethical Code by Dialogue Conferences

HANS DE GEER

I. Object

If your company's moral is being questionned in the media, if you need an ethical code or have to enhance company ethics in other ways – what can you do? Are ethical codes best written by externals, e. g. smart business consultants or the ethical professionals in the churches, or should you try to develop a creed from the inside? In this paper we discuss results and experiences from a major company case, where internal dialogue conferences were used. It involves writing an ethical code and creating processes to promote moral competence.

II. The Company and the Commission

The client is a Swedish insurance company. Different factors had created a need for a formal ethical code. The insurance business is changing, not least as a consequence of internationalization. The company had recently established businesses in Europe and in the US and owned property in several countries. It had recently merged with an other insurance company with quite different scope, tradition and corporate culture, and it had changed its legal status from a mutual insurance company to a joint stock company. Internal statements of policy had focussed on values of economy and profit rather than the care-taking, social aspects of insurance. In a couple of cases the company had recently been harassed in media for having mistreated their clients though, and actually by, strictly following law, rules and contracts.

Management felt a need for restating corporate values in a broader sense. We were therefore approached and got the commission to write an ethical code and to investigate if there already were any local efforts to strengthen the organization's moral competence and to stimulate or initiate such efforts.

III. The Research Program and its Problems

The research program *Ideology and Norms* analyses the relationship between values, work and business. It consists at present of six projects, three of which is more directly adressing business ethics. One is concerned with ethical codes and other moral support structures in Swedish companies, how common they are, what they usually cover and how they work. Another investigates the national characteristics of ethics: are there significative differences of opinion between nationalities? If so, how can they be described and how can they be dealt with? The third project, *Ethics through communication*, is the most relevant here. It assumes that ethics are shaped within different communities and asks what sort of discussions take place concerning ethical questions in companies and organizations, and what characterizes a good moral discussion? Can the prerequisities be created for a good moral discussion in enterprises so that individuals can develop their moral competence?

A number of case studies are outlined in the plans of the project, but none is done so far. The problems of access are always difficult. Ideally you should be in an organization before ethical questions arise as consequences of external events. In the midst of a crises access might prove hard and even unwise. The offer from the insurance company constituted an opportunity for us to follow an organization during the process of formulating its ethical standpoints. It was an opportunity to create the communicative situation, to set the stage for the discussion, to try participative research in order to understand the nature of the moral dialogue.

IV. Theory

Our theoretical points of departure are outlined in our paper to the EBEN research institutes' conference in Hannover 1991.[1] The keyword is moral competence, which can be interpreted as an organizational, not merely individual asset. Moral competence is the knowledge or awareness of moral issues involved in the everyday work and the ability to argue for choices made and alternatives preferred. Moral competence can be seen as a part of the broader social competence which is required in today's working life. The entitlement to moral competence is part of the good social and psychological conditions of work that should be granted every employee.

We maintain, that there are three means of promoting the moral competence. First, individuals can attend courses, read books and discuss ethical questions with their family or friends. Business ethics can also be taught at business schools and economy faculties at universities. Second, within companies the moral competence can be enhanced and supported by structural means. Here we think of ethical codes, ethical committees, ethical responsible bodies and the like. In the organizational structure and in the web of working rules are installed measures to absorb moral uncertainty and to take on the responsibility as long as employees are following the rules and acknowledge the organizational pattern.

All of this is good, but there is the risk that structural measures decay into just formalities. In a turbulent environment, business does not need too rigid formal systems. On the other hand more stability of values might be the very thing needed. The real problem might be how to use

1 T. BRYTTING, H. DE GEER: *Moral Dilemmas and Organization Design*, in: P. KOSLOWSKI (ed.): *Ethics in Economics, Business, and Economic Policy*, Berlin, Heidelberg, New York (Springer) 1992, S. 95–115.

the rules, how to overcome the discrepancy between general rules and the unique situation, where action takes place. Double standards could be a solution to the dilemma. In that case, silence is necessary. In all other cases, moralizing, that is the shaping or memorizing of current values, has to be done in a vivid and participating way. Our third type of means are communicative, dialogue, or "the good conversation", to use the expression of Frederick Bird.[2]

Moral values, we believe, must be formulated in an interplay between people, within the family, the community, the congregation, the nation, within international bodies, and in our case, within the firm. The day to day adoption of values, the very choices of action, the discussion of what is right and what should be avoided, the gossip of scandals as well as the official rewards, all of this forms part of the communicative, moralizing murmur of the workplace. Not being longlived silent flies sitting in the ceilings, it can be difficult for us to follow that moralizing process. For research ends, we will have to look for special events when the moralizing dialogue can be assumed to be louder or more clear than most of the time, or we have to arrange special occasions for our study.

Given these standpoints it was clear, that the process of writing an ethical code had to start with, and aim at, a communicative process, in which the employees concerned were participating. We had, however, no practical experiences from such an undertaking. In principle we had to jump into the cold water with an untested mix of theory and practice. That led us to consider the Scandinavian experience with dialogue. It has its roots in the combination of Habermas' critical theory, Tavistock theory and a Scandinavian tradition of cooperation. We decided to try the conference method, developed and well tested in fieldwork within the LOM-programme *Management, organization and participation*, which was sponsored by The Swedish Work Environment Fund (Arbetsmiljöfonden). A lot of case studies proved organised dialogue to be a useful means to change organizations and working conditions.[3] It has been used primarily, but not exclusively, in blue collar work-places. It has been developed further to deal with gender and influence in organizations.

2 F. BIRD: *The Role of "Good Conversation" in Busniess Ethics*. Monograph from the proceedings of the First Annual James A Waters Colloquium on Ethics in Practice, Boston college, 1990.

3 B. GUSTAVSEN, P. ENGELSTAD: "The Design of Conferences and the Evolving Role of Democratic Dialogue in Changing Working Life", *Human Relations*, 39 (1986), no. 2. For an evaluation, see also the 1992 report by FRIEDER NASCHOLD, Wissenschaftszentrum, Berlin: (titel to be decided)

V. Practice

The formal setting of the dialogue is important. There has got to be acknowledged arenas – time and space – for dialogues, and it is necessary that everyone at the work place is provided with resources to join the dialogue, a right to speak, a language to use, information and respect. The criteria for a good dialogue are the following, according to the LOM researchers:

1. The dialogue is a process of exchange: ideas and arguments move to and fro between the participants.
2. It must be possible for all concerned to participate.
3. This possibility for participating is however not enough. Everybody should also be active. Consequently each participant has an obligation not only to put forth his or her own ideas, but also to let others to contribute their ideas.
4. All participants are equal.
5. Work experience is the basis for participation. This is the only type of experience which, by definition, all participants have.
6. At least some of the experience which each participant has when entering the dialogue must be considered legitimate.
7. It must be possible for everybody to develop an understanding of the issues at stake.
8. All arguments which pertain to the issues and the discussion are legitimate. No argument should be rejected on the ground that it emerges from an illegitimate source.
9. The points, arguments etc, which are to enter the dialogue must be made by a participating actor. Nobody can participate "on paper" only.
10. Each participant must accept that other participants can have better arguments.
11. The work rule, authority etc. of all the participant can be made subject to discussion – no participant is except in this respect.
12. The participant should be able to tolerate an increasing degree of difference of opinion.
13. The dialogue must continuously produce agreements which can provide platforms for practical actions. Note that there is no contradiction between this criterion and the previous one. The major strength of a democratic system compared to all other ones is that it has the benefit of drawing upon a broad range of opinions and

ideas which inform practice, while at the same time being able to make descisions which can gain the support of all participants.[4]

The form of conferences are quite strictly designed, but their content depends on the participants themselves. Participants should ideally come from four different work-places and they should be interested in the subject-matter, representative for their fellows and collegues back home and together the participants from each workplace should have the mandate to decide on programs for change. The most important asset for participation is the own work experience that every participant brings into the dialogue. Sometimes, however, someone might lack the proper language – knowledge might be tacit and everyday expressions might not always do in these meta-discussions – or the necessary self-esteem to express his experience. The conferences are therefore designed in order to cope with this problem.

Conferences usually start at lunchtime the first day and are closed at lunch the second. They consist of a series of group discussions, where the compositions of the groups are varied. First the participants meet in homogenous groups, that is, for example, workers from all companies in one group, foremen in another, middle managers in the third and the executives in the fourth. That is a way of starting to formulate common experiences, to provide everyone with a language. Then the groups are reformed. Next the workers from one company meet foremen from another, middle managers from yet another etc. That is a way to start discussions over the barriers of hierarchy, without invoking the everyday inequal structure of influence. Problems can be discussed more frankly and solutions suggested more daringly. At last the partcipants from each workplace get together to formulate a program, or at least some projects for change, which is acceptable to all of them, which they think is acceptable to the people back home and which they therefore commit themselves to realize before a given date. Each group discussion is summarized in a plenary session, where each group has to report their discussions and results, e. g. by a diagraph. That provides transparency of the procedure and a commitment to what has been said.

In order to formulate the ethical code for the company we decided to combine our theoretical assumptions with this conference method to make sure that the moral experiences of the employees were the very base of the code and to secure their cooperation and commitment in the undertaking.

4 B. GUSTAVSEN: *Dialogue and Development,* van Gorcum, Assen/ Maastricht/ Swedish Center for Working Life, Stockholm 1992

VI. Planning the Conferences

The company appointed a steering committee for the project, involving the president and CEO, the vice president for communications, another senior vice president, one director of the board and the researchers from the FAinstitute. The division, in which the project was to be carried out, was represented by its president. All in all, 130 people from the division took part in the conferences. The staff was now reinforced with a researcher with experience from LOM for the conferences, and with a director of the board in the actual writing. The time schedule for the project was set – we could spend about three months before we were to report and present at least an outline to an ethical code.

The time for the project was squeezed by the unusually long Christmas holidays and by another encompassing project going on in the division, which aimed at anchoring a new set of company values among the employees.

We started talking to key persons in the division to learn to know the company and to let them know what we were doing. The practicalities of planning the four conferences, i. e. reserve hotels etc, were left to a company manager. We did not take on any responsibility for housing, meals and the like.

VII. The First Conferences

Four conferences took place within a period of three weeks. We labelled the four sessions as follows:

1. What is the "good" company?
2. Which are the principle obstacles in realizing the "good" company?
3. Which are the actual obstacles at your work-place to realize it?
4. Indicate in terms of projects what you can do in order to get closer to the ideal!

The structure of a conference is given. The participants provide the content of the discussion and have the initiative in planning the projects. The conference leaders should restrict themselves to procedure, to maintain and guard the principles of the dialogue. The first two conferences were no successes, the second two turned out better or even good. What happened?

The first two conferences demonstrated that the procedure did not give the necessary energy to the conference. The various group discussions were often interesting, but without focus, in some cases more critical to the whole idea of a conference on their professional ethics. We, the leaders, remained, as was the intention, quite passive, waiting for the participants to take over the process. But they did not and virtually nothing happened. No value was created in the conferences. Participating managers, some of whom participated in both conferences, became increasingly critical and even reported their mistrust up the line. We had to evaluate our methods.

VIII. Halftime Evaluation of the Method

We identified a number of factors that could have influenced the outcome of the conferences. Some of them could be classified as our mistakes in planing, other as our perceptions of characteristics of the company, which required certain modifications in the procedure.

Wrong Expectations

The preparatory process was unsatisfacory. That was partly due to lack of time (Christmas, other concurrent "drives"), partly to our misjudgements. We knew, from other experience, that it was crucial to meet in advance with everyone who was to attend a conference, in order to explain the purposes and the method. Against better knowledge we accepted management's suggestion to let the participants be formally called to the conferences without face-to-face information. Participants came to the conferences with wrong or unrealistic expectations (that we would tell them about business ethics) or without any preparations or preunderstanding at all. With more time for preparation the problem could be solved.

Standing Accused

Summoned to a conference on business ethics, to meet external "experts", the participants felt accused of having a bad moral or behaving immorally. Naturally they took a negative or defensive stand from the beginning. It was not until we started to point out the non-personal reasons for a recurrent moral dialogue, that they accepted the situation. But they remained quite passive, expecting us to tell them how to argue and how to behave. That the reverse was the real situation they only gradually accepted: that they were expected to express their own moral guidelines and dilemmas. Had we seen the problem in advance it could easily have been coped with, insofar as it concerned our attitude. But there remained the suspicion that top management, in taking the initiative, might believe that rank and file employees needed "a moral rearmament".

Hierarchy

In the concept of development by conferences it is assumed that hierarchy is important. Conferences are therefore designed to short-circuit hierarchy. This did not work. The reasons for this, we believe, are twofold. First, there is here a clear ambition to avoid conflict. There is merely an intent to create family-like relations in the organization. Second, hierarchy is not acknowledged in the company culture in this case. The social self-identification of the employees is merely the same, regardless of their formal position in the company. This is facilitated by the distribution of men and women in the organization, comparatively more men being promoted and comparatively more women in subordinate positions. Differences in hierarchy can thus be perceived as traditional, let be deplorable, differences in gender. This was a more genuine problem, which could not have been avoided by better planning, but one nevertheless had be coped with in the conferences.

Language

In the ordinary, mostly blue collar work-places, the creation or acquiring of a language to express ones experiences gives *per se* a certain energy to the conference. In our case that did not occur. The participants were from the outset very verbal. At face value we accepted that and waited for the discussion to take off. It turned out, however, that they nevertheless were unable of the discussion that we wanted them to get into. They lacked adequate theoretical notions for the ethical discourse. It was not until we had given them the notions, the tools, and shown them that the situation permitted the usage of quite demanding, "big" words, that the dialogue became vivid. This is also a more genuine problem.

Campaign Overload

Other activities going on in the company made participants overloaded. Projects, programmes, campaigns of various kinds had followed upon each other in the division. Again and again the employees had been asked to react, to be creative, to come up with ideas of how to promote change or how to implement the strategies adopted over their heads. Too often they had got no feed-back to their suggestions. They obviously had good reason te believe that these conferences were another fad and that the best they could do was to sit there quietly and wait for a better weather. Any engagement or creativity would certainly be a waste of energy.

Managers' Attitudes

The attitude of managers is crucial to the efforts. In this case the initiative came from top management, and subordinate managers just had to obey orders: there was to be a project on business ethics. The division manager were not necessarily as eager as the CEO to start the process, but he did. Some of the regional managers felt even more bossed about. This feeling was underpinned by their perception of the moral incompetence not being at the base, but at the top of the company hierarchy. As participants in the conferences they had to demonstrate their integrity and question the necessity of the project, thus willingly or unwillingly showing their subordinates that the project was not worth paying much attention to. Without the firm support from managers, demonstrating that the project is seriously meant, the conference method is not likely to give good results. More time spent on preparations could have alleviated, though probably not solved the problem.

IX. The Last Conferences

As mentioned, we gave the standard conference blue-print two chances, but realized – before we heard of the reported criticism – that we had to put some energy in the process. We started to change the conference design. We maintained that experience must be expressed by the participants, but we tried to focus the process. We introduced ethics in a formal lecture. We formally asked participants to compose an ethical code for their company, based on their own experience. The new sequence of sessions became the following:

1. A formal, more theroretical lecture on ethics and a briefing on why ethics have to be reconsidered from time to time in a company.
2. A standard form of ethical code was presented and participants asked to fill it in.
3. Conflicting norms and work routines were discussed, which seemed uncompatible with the ethical code. They had been gathered partly during the previous conferences, partly in a special survey.
4. The prerequisites of a good dialogue were presented and local initiatives and projects were discussed.

In this way we gave the participants more theoretical background. In fact we gave them tools to use in discussing their mutual experience. The last two conferences turned out to be a success, both in terms of participants evaluation and in terms of quality of papers produced. Each session resulted, as mentioned in a overhead projection sheet from each group, which makes 16 sheets from each conference, or a total of about 50 sheets of different content, focus and quality. This constituted, together with our own experiences and notes, the material for the next phase of the project, the writing of the ethical code.

X. Writing a Code

The blueprint for an ethical code, that we provided during the conferences, consisted of four parts:

1. The company's basic values,
2. The company's "mission"
3. The nature of the company's relations to others
4. The rule of conduct for professional work within the actual division.

The company being in the service sector, it was natural to focus on the ethics of relations between client and company, i. e. what restrictions the company should impose on its own action visavi the clients. There was an unanimosity on certain characteristica of the company-client relation. It should be fair, transparent, consistent and businesslike. From this conception of the ideal relations we induced basic values concerning man and society, within which it made sense. The basic values of the firm were a conception of man as equal, responsible and with personal integrity, and a conception of ideal society as being democratic and having a free market economy. These values were based, we concluded, in a common belief among the employees.

Then we tried to establish a common idea of the mission of the company. The employees in the division, it turned out, had often a clear picture of the overall mission and did not hesitate to express it. It was formulated in a number of sentences.

The third part had to do with the company's relations in society, not just to clients but also to subcontractors, local authorities, employees and others. The important issue was if the company by its external and internal relations should promote a ethical behaviour and, if so, in what way that influence could be exercised. We tried to find key words and key notions stated in the records of the group discussions.

The fourth and last part of the code consisted of rules and prescribed routines for the actual division. There existed already an accepted professional code of conduct for the whole business, but it was, as we found out, not very well recognized among the employees in this company. We used it together with the suggestions from the conferences in a new writing, more modern and more adapted to the actual company. Of course, most of it would also other companies subscribe to. The conception of ethical rules, should not be a tool for profilizing the company. But the adherence to the code, the ethical behaviour as such, could on the other hand be an important trait in the company image.

XI. Feed-back Meetings and Actual Status

The suggested code was distributed to the people that had participated in the conferences with a copy of the report we had delivered to the CEO and a list of the problematic praxises that we had identified. The participants has the right to know exactly what had been reported from our meeting and were thus given the opportunity to approve or disapprove of the draft code. We arranged feed back meetings with the personell in each region at their own regional head office. Starting with a close reading of the text of professional code we conducted what can be described as a model "credo challenging seminar".

The reactions among the participants were often polarized between two extremes. Some maintained that the text contained nothing new, nothing that differed from existing praxis and was just a codification of common sense. The other extreme, often demonstrated at the same time, sometimes even by the same persons, was occupied by those who held the text to be just unbelievable, and its intentions unreal or unrealistic and believed that management just could not be serious. The aim of the discussion, then, was to proceed from this starting point to establishing 1) that the code was something more than just common sense, and 2) that it was seriously meant, in fact that it represented a conscious choice by the top management, a choice of a an ethical profile, to be acquired even at a certain cost.

As a rule, the discussions were good and were perceived as fruitful by the participants. The criticism of or the deviating opinions on the proposed text were generally aimed at passuses that seemed too binding or too definite. For instance, promises to do something *immediately*, or *without delay* or to guarantee *the highest possible* level of service were suggested to be changed to expressions like *without undue delay* and *a fair level of service*.

Also, our suggestion that the concept *client* should be introduced to indicate a special relation between the producer and the consumer of the service rendered, was rejected partly because it was felt as strange or unusual, partly because the personell did not want to take on the special responsibilities connected to that relationship.

Now, if top management decided to aim at the higher level of ambition and the different responsibility implied in our earlier suggestions, that would be willingly accepted by the personell. Such a decision would also have an impact on the competitive position of the company in the market and could be used as a means to positionate the company in relation to its competitors. That illustrates both how the code works as a management tool and as a device to construct a company profile.

In our original report we pointed to certain problems in the existing praxis that would arise if the code was adopted. Certain routines, certain service concepts seemed to be more or less difficult to reconcile with the principles expressed in the ethical code. In that situation three solutions can be considered: 1) silence, that is not to confront praxis and theory, which results in an often practical but a bit dangerous situation of double standards, or 2) adopt the wording of the code to praxis with an (implicit) argumentation for its necessity, or 3) change praxis. In fact, all three alternatives have been propagated in the feed-back discussions. In some cases praxis has been changed or is under investigation, in other cases arguments are being gathered to defend praxis and to educate the personell, which of cause is a way to achieve a better moral competence. Silence is in fact chosen if the code is not recognized for all parts of the concern and the companies tranquilly are left to develop their own standards.

Thus, the situation now is the following. A version of the professional code has been presented and accepted by the personell with minor changes. It is now to be scrutinized by the legal advisers of the company and then adopted by top management and an implementation plan, including information and educational efforts, is to be executed. For the more encompassing parts of the code the ambition of top management is to be reformulated, taking into account a thorough reorganization of the concern. Local activities to enhance organizational moral competence by creating better opportunities for internal dialogue exist in some regions but should benefit from the encouragement of a firm statement from the side of the top management that moral competence is to be regarded as important and given a higher priority.

Work has began in the division to use the code, though not yet formally accepted by CEO and Board, as one of three pillars on which to reconstruct the organization of the actual work. Discussions are also held on the possibilities of linking the code to the human resource management program at the corporate level as well as to the overall quality work.

The most important part of the implementation process is to make the moral dialogue an effective asset of the organization's own, not merely a consultants' project. One way of achieving this is to state the responsibility of every manager on all levels to withhold and enhance the moral competence by means of recurring dialogues in the organization. That should be managers' responsibility in the same way as it is their duty to uphold the necessary competence in other respects. It is also something they owe their employees in the same way as they owe them attention to their conditions of work and possibilities of advancement.

XII. Recommendations

Is then the conference method to be recommended in formulating a company creed? Yes, in an overall account we tend to believe so. But it is important not to make the mistakes again. It is necessary to claim the right, the time and the resources to see every participant in advance, even against the managers' will. It is important not to be impressed by people being talkative – they might nevertheless lack the adequate language without which any moral codes are never constructed. On the other hand, properly held, the conferences might provide a support for the efforts of establishing from bottom up an ethical code in the company.

Dialogue conferences are not only vehicles for organizational change or opportunities to trace moral values in an organization. It also gives the participants a training and an experience of *dialogue* as a method. Dialogue is in fact the very process by which moral competence can be achieved and withheld in an organization.

References

BRYTTING, T., DE GEER, H.: *Moral Dilemmas and Organization Design*, in: P. KOSLOWSKI (ed.): *Ethics in Economics, Business, and Economic Policy*, Berlin, Heidelberg, New York (Springer) 1992, S. 95–115.

BIRD, F.: *The Role of "Good Conversation" in Business Ethics*. Monograph from the proceedings of the First Annual James A. Waters Colloquium on Ethics in Practice, Boston college, 1990.

GUSTAVSEN, B., ENGELSTAD, P.: "The Design of Conferences and the Evolving Role of Democratic Dialogue in Changing Working Life", *Human Relations*, 39 (1986), no. 2. For an evaluation, see also the 1992 report on the LOM program by FRIEDER NASCHOLD, Wissenschaftszentrum, Berlin.

GUSTAVSEN, B.: *Dialogue and Development*, van Gorcum, Assen/ Maastricht/ Swedish Center for Working Life, Stockholm 1992.

Part Three

Post-communist Experiences

Chapter 6

Control, Communication and Ethics The Dilemma of the Modernization-theory in Central and Eastern Europe

LÀSZLÒ FEKETE

The Project of modernity has been the key issue in the social and economic thinking in Central and Eastern Europe for, at least, a half-century. From a pragmatic point of view, the socialist economic system was also an attempt to take the challenge of this Western European paradigm. Leaving aside the ideological justification of the socialist system, the project of modernization in order to catch up with the speed of the Western European social and economic development offered the most powerful argument to defend the legitimacy of its historical existence. The socialist economic system was collapsed but the old paradigm of modernity has managed to survive this upheaval. The recent Central and Eastern European governments want to modernize the economy and society again, as if the near fulfillment of modernity is the only way to solve the global problems of this region, and as if the process of modernization is the only track of history. The question must be raised whether the new-old attempt of fulfilling modernity is anachronistic or not? Partly because the societies of Western Europe have left behind this paradigm or, at least, the basic values of modernity/modernization have been profoundly reconsidered. Therefore the project of modernity in the societies of Central and Eastern Europe continues in a quite extraordinary historical situation because its basic values should be fulfilled and, at the same time, surpassed as that happened to the Western part of Europe. The question is whether the societies of Central and Eastern Europe can successfully take the challenge of fulfilling as well as surpassing the basic values of modernity in the economy and society, I shall briefly review the circumstances which have led to this peculiar historical-situation.

As you know well, in the project of modernity the philosophical values of the Enlightenment were secularized. The main components of those values as the idea of subject, the contractual and, later on, constitutional notion of society, and progress were anthropological, political, and historical. The rights of subjects to act freely and rationally in the economy and society are especially substantial from the point of view of how just economic system and moral society can be brought about. In other words, the rational actions of subject in the economy and society became a norm as well as the measure of freedom and moral justness. This is the reason why the project of modernity is usually analyzed as the transformation of the abstract philosophical ideas on man and society into the practical norms and measures of the social and economic action.

For the freedom of the rational individual action became the norm and the measure, this principle changed the social and economic space of the individual participation in and contribution to forming a just economic system and the moral society. Briefly, man started to go after the idea of a developmental history in the project and the result of this own individual actions, in other words, in the wordly and temporal horizon of the economy and society. The project and the result of his own individual actions are frequently manifested in the only material progress. At least, there was a strong conviction that the moral society can be formed by means of a just economic system. After all, "Nature speaks to man in the language of economy". In this way, the freedom of the individual social and economic action and the realization of its moral end are somehow limited by a world of universal scarcity. The world of universal scarcity sets the limit of the free acquisition of goods and political rights, and ultimately, the full realization of the moral end of the individual action. The creed of the world of universal scarcity and therefore the necessity of the restraints of the freedom of the acting subject became an axiomatic truth, especially, in the first stage of the process of modernization. However these liberal political creeds stimulated the growing criticism which, instead of following the different philosophical anthropological approach, argued against the creed of the world of universal scarcity and the necessity of the restraints of the freedom of the acting subject in the very same theoretical framework. Both theoretical approaches took the axiomatic truths of modernity for granted even if its social time dimension, to wit, whether the moral values of modernity can be temporarily limited or not for the purpose of the future achievements, is entirely different.

The contradiction existed from the outset between the moral foundation of modernity has managed to save its dynamic character in the philosophical thinking as well as in the social and economic practice for centuries. This contradiction which in my opinion can not and should not be eliminated and which is, of course, a scandal from a well-established philosophical point of view always gives new impetus for the society even today. Because the modernity is regarded as the form and manner of the social and economic action and, at the same time, as the norm of the evaluation of its result from the viewpoint of moral justness this contradiction assures its dynamic character.

Somehow it is quite amazing that the basic values of a pure (but not innocent) philosophical movement which certainly did not originate from any social and economic practice and did not possess any wordly image step by step sedimented as the moral consequences of the just and rational human action in the long process of modernization. As I have emphasized above, the contradiction between, so to say, the universe of moral values and the values of the wordly practice explains us the dynamic character of modernity. Namely, the project of modernity in its unachieved status sets some limit for the freedom of the individual social and economic action, at the same time, this limit can be always reconsidered and refuted on its very same philosophical basis.

The intellectual movements of Central and Eastern Europe sometimes feebly communicated with their counterparts in Western Europe. Therefore the societes in our region have quite different understanding about the meaning of modernity. First of all, modernity usually does not mean a project embedded in the creative participation of the acting subject to form a just economic system and the moral society by means of enlarging the social and economic space of the rational action, securing the free communication among the different strata of society, enabling every individual member of society to act morally, etc. Modernity is taken as a ready-made project or rather a blueprint that came from the historical necessity. Therefore it merely needs subjects who under the control of the state follow out the instruction of history in the process of modernization. This process of modernization is the age of the earthly suffering for the society which must be endured as the decades of the migration in the desert until arriving the promised land. For this reason, it is not wise to object against the constraints of the freedom of the acting subject and the lack of a just economic system and the moral society during this process because those institutions can be only formed after the fulfillment of modernity. In this way, the social time dimension of this understanding of modernity is a static phenomenon; the individuals are not in command of the historically structured time of modernity. The feasibility of the just economic system and the moral society appears only beyond the horizon of the social and economic presence.

Modernity in Central and Eastern Europe is frequently pictured as a hierarchic and normative set of values or rather prescriptions for the individuals and different social groups in the economy and society which belong to the deep-structure of history. Therefore the schedule of history and not dialogically achieved social consensus among the individuals and different social groups determines the possibility and the limit of the freedom of the individual social and economic action. It must be said that the social sciences have detached the very meaning of modernity from its own cultural, philosophical origin and made it as the objective historical process controlled by the state. This distorted meaning of modernity has determined the forms of communication, the manner of speech about the possibilities and the limits of the freedom of the individual and social action in the process of modernization for a long time. This dogmatic manner of speech has prevented society from emhasizing moral issues and from reaching any dialogically achieved consensus concerning development, social participation, the distribution of wealth, the role of the individuals etc until now.

I have began with the review of the project of modernity, its distorted meaning, and the dogmatic manner of speech about it in the societies of Central and Eastern Europe. The eloquence of the old official social science is not so interesting subjext itself. It is quite obvious, however, that there will be a scientific paradigm which is intended to defend the so-called enlightened absolutism of the Central and Eastern European regimes and to justify the necessity of the bureaucratic control of the centralized state over the freedom of the individual and social action for some ambiguous purpose of the general interest in the future even if this kind of scientific paradigm will be less and less defendable by rational arguments. As the recent discussion about the future economic and social development in our region shows us, it can not be expected that this distorted meaning of modernity will die out soon.

The real question is whether the societies of Central and Eastern Europe can get rid of that project of modernity which is understood as the only – even if painful – way of the rational allocation of the human and material resources by means of the bureaucratic control of the centralized state in order to catch up with the speed of the Western European social and economic development as if it has happened to the societies in Central and Eastern Europe in the last four or five decades? If the social and economic thinking in this region will become free from the old paradigm of how to modernize the economy and society on what kind of values the individual and social action can be founded? Can the moral concern be ignored for the purpose of the rational allocation of the human and material resources, at least, in short term, again which is in return the basic precondition to form a just economic system and the moral society? What insight seems to be still absent today is that there is no any chronological order between economic rationality and morality. (As Berthold Brecht ironically stated: "Erst kommt das Fressen, dann kommt die Moral.")

I do not think, of course, that the societies of Western Europe have brought to perfection their economic and social institutional structure. But at least, their institutional structure works and day by day overcomes the social and economic conflicts by means of promoting dialogues among the different interest groups of society. In other words the social and economic system, and its functional elements – market, the pluralistic structure of the political institutions, the media of the free communication etc. – can make the regular correction in case of the conflicting interests in the economy and society. This regular correction never results to the massive deconstruction of the functional elements of the whole economic and political framework as it has happened in the long political practice of the Central and Eastern European societies for many decades. In our region, the history over and over tried to be started, again. Whether one is the faithful advocate of the so-called "piecemeal-reform" or not, the different social strata of the postmodern political system seem to accept the dialogical solutions of the conflicting interests in the economy and society. In return, the postmodern political system does not endanger the very existence of the alternative forms of the social integration and the non-politically organized Öffentlichkeit. The most remarkable in the recent trend of the Western European development is that the main concern of the individuals is the "Life-world", the freedom of communication, culture etc. Less and less persons believe that the personality could be reformed by the profound change of the great social and economic systems. The rationality of these systems, the rational social and economic actions of the individuals and different social groups never lead to the perfectibility of life as it is thought in our societies. The contingency of life, person, and dialogue does not beg for any rational arrangement supervised by the bureaucratic control of the state. Here history seems to be in standstill, or at least, the real story takes place in "Life-world" and in person. Maybe, this historical situation reflects the recent understanding that the European culture can not be rectified by means of the logic of political power.

LÀSZLÒ FEKETE

Today, the societies of Central and Eastern Europe do not offer too much chance for those who can not or do not want to participate in the power-game of the recent social and economic transformation like kids, pensioners, workers, peasants, the unemployed, the schoolteachers, women, intellectuals etc. In the recent economic and social transformation the "Life-world" as the key issue of the future success of this transformation is left out of consideration. History still means the rule of the objective historical laws over the "Life-world". As a consequence of the strong belief in the distorted meaning of modernity in the societies of Central and Eastern Europe, man can hardly understand the importance of his/her personal participation in the process of modernization. The logic of political power in the past decades endeavoured to eliminate the contradiction between the presence of the individuals and the rule of the historical laws over their participation by means of the totalization of history. The elimination of this mentioned contradiction meant that the individuals were not at the disposal of their own "Life-world", culture, and dialogue. The myths of the different modernization theories in our region helped to conserve the command of the political power over the rational allocation of the human and material resources and subordinate the interests of the civil society to the depersonalized project of modernity. It is quite certain that the recent social and economic transformation of our region can not be successful if this process takes place in the old framework and under the bureaucratic control of the centralized state. The logic of old political power, however, is not entirely alien from the practice of the newly elected regimes in Central and Eastern Europe. The economic hardship which is supposed to legitime the bureaucratic control over the human and material resources and the strict state-regulation is frequently used as an argument in excuse of the continuity of this old political practice. In spite of the modest performance of the newly elected governments and their attempt of controlling the process of the social and economic transformation sometimes in a quite authoritarian manner what is very promising is that these governments have to learn the strong pragmatic attitude of these societies which are not ready to give up even an inch from its painfully achieved freedom. It seems to me the leadership of these new political establishments is quite hesitant to take an interest in emphasizing the ethical aspects of this historical transformation. Therefore, as far as I can see, our recent task in business ethics is to make the civil society be aware of and be able to express the importance of the ethical issues in the economy and society.

References

DAHRENDORF, R.: *Betrachtung über die Revolution in Europa,* Stuttgart 1990.
HABERMAS, J.: *Der philosophische Diskurs der Moderne*, Frankfurt/Main 1985.
KOSLOWSKI, P.: *Wirtschaft als Kultur. Wirtschaftskultur und Wirtschaftsethik in der Postmoderne*, Wien 1989.
POLÁNYI, K.: *The great transformation*, London 1944.
VAJDA, M.: *Eastern Europe and the Postmodern*, manuscript 1991.

Chapter 7

Actual Problems of Ethical Business for Small Entrepreneurs in Czechoslovakia

LIDMILA NĚMCOVÁ

I. Small Business Development in Czechoslovakia

The business in Czechoslovakia underwent during the World War II and, in particular, after 1948, a complex development. It is necessary to mention the shock caused by the Munich agreement in 1938 and the following years of Nazi occupation and war, the repercussions of which could not be remedied during the short relatively favourable period after the war (1945–1948). Whereas the post-war developments were not essentially different from those taking place in other highly developed European countries, after 1948 the so-called socialisation of any business took place. Private enterprises were abolished and all business activities were transferred to the State and cooperative sectors. The whole economic life was subject to central planning and command management.

Many sectors – as foreign trade – were organised as a State monopoly. Only one subject was responsible for foreign trade activities, the State and its organisations created for this purpose. Foreign trade activities were gradually redirected towards the trade with members of the Council of Mutual Economic Assistance.

Only since the end of the 1989 substantial changes have taken place in the economic, social and political life of the country. These changes have made it possible to start a gradual transformation towards market economy. It should be emphasized that small business activities in Czechoslovakia have had a strong tradition, as distinct from other countries of the previous socialist block. In spite of the fact that activities of small private businesses were repeatedly suppressed, it can be expected that reconstitution of this sector in Czechoslovakia will not take too long, and that by the end of 2000 commercial activities could assume their role in Europe. Already before 1990 a number of people had been active in foreign trade, who had the possibility to acquire the corresponding know-how and learn foreign languages, obtain experiences, etc. These people are able to adapt themselves relatively fast to the changed conditions.

II. Barriers to Further Development

To achieve the renaissance of small business in Czechoslovakia, it is necessary to overcome various obstacles. A systematic-enumeration of them can be made according to different criteria. According to horizons of time of their possible removal or surmounting, it is possible to distinguish short-, medium- and long-term obstacles. Such a distinction makes it possible to concentrate on the removal of those barriers which can be removed quickly while not losing sight of significiant problems of a strategic nature the solution of which can be expected in a relatively more distant future, but which must be, nevertheless, systematically addressed, starting from now. Any delay could cause difficulties in the future.

Important obstacles concern the financial, tax, real estate, legislation, and other areas. Specific problems are those of know-how, training, new image of cooperatives etc. The special research, based on a questionnaire in various environments, led to a surprising conclusion that it is the absence of ethics in entrepreneurship which has been very frequently mentioned as the main barrier to entrepreneurship.

III. Problems of Ethics in Small Business

The change of the political regime brought about many problems. Besides positive developments (enabling – above all – to initiate the transformation of the Czechoslovak economy) negative symptoms started to emerge and grow that grossly interfere with the development of ethics in the small business environment. Several examples can serve to illustrate the situation:

- breach of compliance with concluded contracts (in respect of price, quality, quantity, delivery terms), in particular in case of oral contracts etc.
- seemingly low prices without informing the client about deficient quality (lapsed guarantee periods, inferior quality, indeed waste products)
- impossibility to submit claims in respect of small businesses
- lack of hygiene in transport from the producer to the client,
- lack of business culture (street selling)
- disobliging attitudes towards clients
- chasting (weight, price, giving back change etc.)
- disinformation in advertisements

All these symptoms reflect disproportionate efforts to become rich in a very short time and with minimum effort. A widespread view prevails that trade is an area providing better possibility for enrichment than other sectors (production, other services). Extreme cases are on the boundary line with criminal delicts. Such activities can be of individual nature but various mafia activities can be encountered as well. Such people take advantage of the still existing gaps in the legislation and of further difficulties that are typical for the period of transformation (lack of inspection and control, reduced capacity of police, insufficient penalties and repression measures in cases of gross of low, etc.). No such measures are applied as withholding the licence or prohibition of further activities.

It should be mentioned that some foreign "enterpreneurs" participated actively in these phenomena. Some of them came with the first wave of establishing contacts with unhonest intentions. They wanted to take advantage of lack of experience of their potential trading partners.

IV. Ethical Problems Between Entrepreneurs and the Interests of the Society as a Whole

The disrespect of general welfare and benefit of the society as a whole is a further negative feature which can seriously impair the development of small businesses. Supplies of new products to the market or provision of new or improved services should take account of the need to maintain adequate price levels, which the clients can afford with reasonable profit margins. Sometimes shop-keepers change their stock with respect to highest possible profit without taking into account the need of local population. Evidently, market research is missing with respect of existing income levels. As a consequence there are several areas where basic needs are not met in such products as bread, milk and other foodstuffs, paper products, near to schools, various basic services, such as cleaning, laundering etc. The attitude of the new private entrepreneurs has distorted the network of the existing shops and services. Some of the entrepreneurs who have acquired the existing shops in auctions do not respect the developments that have taken place in the past and the situations existing in certain areas (social structure of the population, new residential districts, networks of large selfservices etc). The descendents of the previous owners who are now eligible for restitution of property very frequently encounter problems – whether to revert to the situation existing forty years ago, or to engage in activities for which they have no training, traditions or adequate personal attitudes.

In longer perspective only honest businessmen with viable business plans can succeed and establish a network of solid shops with adequate culture of sales. These businessmen should be aware of the fact that one of the basic prerequisites for success is good image. It is necessary to promote professional pride and integrity and the satisfaction to be derived from good performance, both on the part of the entrepreneurs and their employees.

Training focussed on ethical principles and their promotion cannot be restricted to small entrepreneurs. The general principles should become part of general education and of an educational campaign, aimed at all citizens. Small entrepreneurs can assume an exemplary role and stand in the forefront. Of course they would expect to obtain an adequate protection against their business partners and clients who might not be prepared to adhere to these principles (protection against blackmail, theft, endangering personal security etc.). In a dishonest environment it is very difficult to promote honesty, integrity and decent behaviour.

VI. Conclusions Concerning Ethics in Business Activities

To overcome the problems referred to, it is necessary:

- to promote a sound entrepreneurial environment, governed by high ethical levels,
- to relate ethical standards to laws and regulations and impose effective penalties for breach of law,
- to create a public understanding for the concepts of honest business and keep profiteers at a distance from honest entrepreneurs,
- to relate training of ethics to people from recent history who could serve as ideals and take advantage of experience gained from Czechoslovak entrepreneurs who succeeded abroad and from foreign entrepreneurs who established their businesses in Czechoslovakia (emphasizing their ethical principles and attitudes),
- to propose to foreign partners to conduct public relations and other activities showing possible solutions to ethical problems (ways and means of solving disputes, activities undertaken by Chambers of Commerce etc.),
- to ask foreign partners to provide assistance in disclosing and exposing dishonest behaviour of entrepreneurs, both Czechoslovak and foreign (Chambers of Commerce, Federations of trades, entrepreneurs and cooperatives – all of them could be active in this report).

The effort of actual EBEN meeting to discuss specific problems concerning the countries – former members of the so-called "Eastern bloc" – is to be highly appreciated. We hope that the intensification of our contacts with EBEN and with its broad experiences will make a considerable contribution for introducing systematically ethical principles into business activities in all these countries.

Chapter 8

God and Profit

V. R. Rokitiansky

On the ancient roots of modern anti-business attitudes in the post-Communist Russian society.[1]

Modern forms of market economy which have proved to be efficient in many countries with most different historic backgrounds are difficult and painful to establish themselves on the Russian soil. For many Russians the new business class is something alien and hostile. And their feeling is not so much envy as hate; their attitude is not one of competition, it is one of denial. In the situation of social non-acceptance the business itself too often takes a cynical if not a criminal image.

A most common explanation for this phenomenon traces it to the ignorance of Russian population, to its incapability to understand the advantages of market economy as a result of the seventy years Communist brain-washing. This explanation is partly valid but superficial and probably biased. It is rooted in the uncritical acceptance of the ideology of optimistic capitalism with its apology of pursuing riches ("making money" as a popular americanism states it) and belief in the automatic salutary value of competition. Our approach, on the contrary, is based on

---

1 The perception of money as something filthy is unerasable from a Russian mind. Marina Tsvetayeva
How hard is for them that trust in riches to enter into the Kingdom of God.
Mk. 10.24

the evident observation that Russian anti-business mentality is much older than Communism in Russia. One should just recall that Russian literature which pictured a series of heroes and righteous people have presented *not a single* image of a businessman that would be more or less morally attractive. The epigraphs suggest that there was some kind of relatedness between the anti-mercantilism of Russian non-religious intelligentsia and Christian other-wordliness. The communists have just exploited this peculiarity of the Russian mind.

The above considerations form a basis for the following RESEARCH AND DEVELOPMENT PROJECT. The RESEARCH part of the project presupposes three directions of research. The historical one – to investigate the genesis of Russian opposition to business. The working hypothesis traces roots of the phenomenon in the following.

I. The Research Project

1. Christian Ethics, Especially its Orthodox Brand

It seems clear that such features as enrichment or competition (which is, plainly speaking, an effort to become richer than others) do pose a problem before a Christian mind. And this problem is one that was being historically solved in struggle and labours. There is a long distance passed between the Early Christian and medieval ideal of poverty and the "In God we trust" on an American dollar, between the prohibition of usuary and modern bank system. On the way a Protestant "theology of business" was developed, the one which has been analysed later by M. Weber.

As for the Orthodox Christianity one could present plenty of evidence of hostility to business and to strivings for enrichment as well as of some intense controversy over the question in Church circles. The famous 16th century dispute between *Nestiazhately* (those who were against monasteries accumulating riches) and *Stiazhately* (those who considered this to be a proper way of strengthening the Church) is a prominent example of the latter (it is worth mentioning that the dispute was over communal property of the Church and that both sides cherished monastic poverty).

A search for Russian solutions of the Christian antinomic view of business brings us also face to face with an interesting phenomenon of the Old Believers' capitalism which was very successful in a short period of the end of XIX century to 1917. The most peculiar feature of this phenomenon was a combination of intense piety and conservatism in the church matters with technological modernism. (A kind of similar development could be pointed to in modern Japan). It is worth mentioning probably that there was a value system with Russian business men of the time which put industry and trade much higher than banking (making money out of money).

2. Peasant Communal Values

The antiindividualistic mentality of Russian *mir* (commune) and of its probable offspring *artel* (a family-like team of workers) have greatly slowed down and shaped the development of capitalism in Russia and have the growing of Socialist ideas and ways of life on the Russian soil much easier.

3. Military and Nobility Values

In Russia as in any feudal society a gentleman was rather squeamish toward money-making. And in the best of nobility this snobbish despise of money was transformed into a genuine lofty-mindedness, care for spirituel matters and common good rather than for personal well-being (this being facilitated of course in most cases by inherited economically secure position).

And now one should just try to imagine what an enormous anti-business, anti-bourgeois complex was characteristic for Russian intelligentsia who inherited all the above mentioned values!

Ethico-phenomenological research – to probe and investigate the modern Russian mind on what is to it the true sense of money, work, business, competition and the like, on what is really valued, envied, denied or feared.

We can give only some guesses on what themes this research would focused upon: the complementary dignity of active and contemplative attitudes, business as doing things, as transforming chaos into cosmos as opposed to mere making money, money as a means to realise to creative projects and to help others etc. (It should be clear that we do not claim

Russian people to bother about all these lofty things instead of striving for personal well-being. We speak about what is considered, not always explicitly, to be *proper* values. Just as probably the proper sense of the "American dream" is the dream of equality, of equal right to happiness).

Sociological and socio-psychological research of the ways, motives and habits of the new Russian business class.

II. The Development Project

The DEVELOPMENT part of the project is considered as the realistic way of solving the urgent and difficult problems of making Russian people and Russian business friends by influencing both sides. Our point is that the task of establishing a modern market economy in Russia cannot be considered a purely technological and educational one. What is also needed is a spiritual work of myth-making. A myth must be created of business as noble, morally and aesthetically attractive, socially praised activity.

Myth is multifunctional. There are several areas it could be used in and thereby there is the task of adjusting the myth to the needs of each area.

1. Myth as Image

Myth as an *image*. That means the image of a businessman presented to the society. The task of creating such image of the business class as a whole and of individual businessmen is easiest for the businessmen to understand and support. It could be a variety of images depending on personality types and other conditions.

2. Myth as Ideal

Myth as an *ideal*. What would you tell to your adolescent son of your business if you wish him to follow you? This aspect of the myth of a businessman has very important pedagogical implications.

3. Myth as Meaning

Myth as *meaning*. This is a complex of motives, implications and references which are necessary to a businessman himself to see his own activity as *meaningful*. This aspect is of prior importance for psychotherapists who would be asked for help by businessmen.

The above mentioned topics were first stated and discussed by a group of researchers, artists and businessmen in the fall, 1991 within the framework of the annual program "The Renaissance" and the Moscow festival "Business Russia". An exhibition on the pre-revolutionary Russian businessmen was an integral part of the said festival with several parts disclosing different features of the image of a businessman at his best:

- Businessman as a creative personality
- Business is a family business
- One who sees profit where others see nothing
- Businessman as a designer transforming his surroundings
- What shall I leave behind?
- Being alone: philosophizing on business

List of Contributors

LARS BERGKVIST is a doctoral student at the Department of Economic Psychology at the Stockholm School of Economics.

TOMAS BRYTTING has a Ph.D. in Business Administration, from the Stockholm School of Economics. At present, he works at the FA Institute in Stockholm. His research has been in the field of organization theory; especially on the relation between technology and organization, and on organization problems in small firms. Present research includes a survey of moral support structures in Sweden, and also a number of case-studies of how moral values are developed and reproduced in organizations. His interest is focused on the communicative character of organizations. He has published two books, a dozen articles and co-authored four books.

Dr. LÁSZLÓ FEKETE was educated in history, economic history and sociology at Budapest, Jena and Binghamton, New York. He was a fellow of Central and Eastern European Research Center and of Fernand Braudel Center from 1981 to 1992. At present he is Associate Professor in Philosophy at Budapest University of Economic Sciences. His research interests are in deontological ethics, hermeneutics and social philosophy. His essays are published in *The Hungarian Review of Philosophy, The Philosophical Observer, The Review of Economics, The Business Ethics*, and many others.

HANS DE GEER, PhD, is professor of business and work life history at Stockholm University and researcher at the FA Institute. There he is the director of the research programme Ideology and Norms. His own research includes various aspects of contemporary and business history, industrial relations, and business ethics and ideology. He is the author of many books and articles. In English he has recently published *The Rise and Fall of the Swedish Model* (1992).

HENK VAN LUIJK is Professor of Ethics and Business Ethics at Nijenrode University, The Netherlands Business School and at the University of Groningen, The Netherlands. He is chairman of EBEN, the European Business Ethics Network, and a member of the Editorial Board of *Business Ethics. A European Review*. He has been a Visiting Scholar at Bentley College and at The Fletcher School of Law and Diplomacy of Tufts University during the Fall Semster of 1991. He has published three books, and over sixty articles, many of them in Dutch, in scholary and professional journals.

DR. LIDMILA NEˇMCOVÁ has been working in the department of small business at the Economic University in Prague. She has been the first to introduce Business Ethics into regular courses. Member of the EBEN, working also with various international and national research teams and for several charity and non-profit organizations.

VERNER C. PETERSEN. Cand. Scient. et Dr. Phil. Lecturer at the Department of Organization and Management, The Aarhus School of Business, Aarhus, Denmark. Present research includes the project "Ethics as a substitute for regulation and control", part of a joint project supported by the Social Science Research Council in Denmark. His research interests include: Ethical issues in decision making; understanding and explaining the process of change in relation to values and ethical rules; the diffusion of ethical and unethical behaviour in organizations and in society; and the relation between the public and the private. His publications include: *Planlaegning of Samfundsudvikling - fra 30'erne til idag.* 3 volumes. Stockholm: Nordplan, Nordiska Institutet för Samhällsplanering, 1985; *Etik*. Herning: systime, 1991.

VLADIMIR ROKITIANSKY is president of the PUT-cooperative, which is a Moscow-based private company, engaged in the organisation of exhibitions and the publishing of books on Russian history.

Springer-Verlag and the Environment

We at Springer-Verlag firmly believe that an international science publisher has a special obligation to the environment, and our corporate policies consistently reflect this conviction.

We also expect our business partners – paper mills, printers, packaging manufacturers, etc. – to commit themselves to using environmentally friendly materials and production processes.

The paper in this book is made from low- or no-chlorine pulp and is acid free, in conformance with international standards for paper permanency.

MIX
Papier aus verantwortungsvollen Quellen
Paper from responsible sources
FSC® C105338

If you have any concerns about our products,
you can contact us on
ProductSafety@springernature.com

In case Publisher is established outside the EU,
the EU authorized representative is:
Springer Nature Customer Service Center GmbH
Europaplatz 3, 69115 Heidelberg, Germany

Printed by Libri Plureos GmbH
in Hamburg, Germany